Why You're DUMB, SICK & BROKE . . .

Why You're DUMB, SICK & BROKE . . .

And How to Get SMART, HEALTHY & RICH!

RANDY GAGE

WILEY

John Wiley & Sons, Inc.

For general information on our other products and services or for technical support, please contact our Customer Care Department within the United States at (800) 762-2974, outside the United States at (317) 572-3993 or fax (317) 572-4002.

Wiley also publishes its books in a variety of electronic formats. Some content that appears in print may not be available in electronic books. For more information about Wiley products, visit our web site at www.wiley.com.

ISBN-13: 978-0-470-04931-0
ISBN-10: 0-470-04931-6

Printed in the United States of America.

10 9 8 7 6 5 4 3 2 1

For the one who guides me, nurtures me,
loves me unconditionally, and brings me joy

Contents

Acknowledgments

There is always a great team of people behind great books. If this book is not great, I alone hold the blame, because I most certainly had a great team to assist me.

My long-time assistant, Lornette Browne, serves as my anchor, keeping me on target, on schedule, and on purpose. She is a blessing.

Vicki McCown did the initial editing with discernment, intelligence, and care, protecting the integrity of the message, keeping my true voice, but ensuring that you the reader can discover the personal meaning here for you.

Matthew Holt and the team from John Wiley & Sons, Inc., are responsible for what you hold in your hands. Matt had a vision for the kind of book the world needed and felt I was the guy to write it.

When it came time to discuss purpose, philosophy, and principles, I had the extraordinary benefit of critical thinkers Bob Burg, Ian Percy, Larry Winget, and Eric Worre.

I am grateful to you all!

CHAPTER 1

Memes and Manipulation: The Battle for Control of Your Mind

■ ■ ■

The Forces Aligned to Keep You Dumb, Sick, and Broke

■ ■ ■

It was that thin line between Saturday night and Sunday morning. I had just returned from an evening at a club. As I parked on the street and got out of my car, a tall stranger bounded up to me. I figured he probably wanted to bum a cigarette or ask directions.

I didn't notice the gun until it was too late.

Turns out the guy was a crackhead desperate for his next fix. This was the eighties, the "wild west" days of Miami and the advent of the crack epidemic, when we were overrun by petty criminals from the Mariel boatlift and the infamous Cocaine Cowboys. South Beach, where I lived, sat at the epicenter of drug activity.

And I was about to become the next statistic. . . .

The guy held the gun to my temple, and his eyes glassed over as though looking right through me. A white Pontiac Fiero pulled up behind us, apparently waiting for my assailant.

Although I practiced martial arts, this situation didn't call for physical defense. The gun remained pointed at my brain, and I knew that if you get shot there, you're done. Even if you're not dead, you're dead. I had no idea whether the accomplice in the car had another gun. (I found out later he did.) And, of course, he could just run me over if he wanted to.

So I elected to try and calm down my attacker, give him my money, and steer the incident to a peaceful resolution. Which works a lot better if you have more than $7 in your pocket! Since a rock of crack cocaine cost five bucks in those days, I kept telling him to take the money, get himself a rock, and we'd just forget about the whole thing. But he wasn't buying that, insisting I had more money and I'd better hand it over.

I kept trying to rationally explain that the seven bucks was all the money I had on me, and he should just take it and get to the crack house. I pointed out why he didn't want the situation to escalate, with probable repercussions being arrest, felony charges, and prison. Of course, crackheads are not known for their rational thinking . . .

Finally, he told me to get back in my car. I don't know how or why, but I knew that if I did get in the car, I wouldn't come out alive. So I refused.

"You have my money, and here are the car keys. You can have the car, but I'm not getting in it. Just take the money, get a rock, I'll walk away, and we'll forget this ever happened."

We were standing under the periphery of a streetlight's glow. I kept slowly edging back toward the bright light in the event someone might drive by or look out from an apartment window. I could see him getting jumpier by the second. The driver of the Fiero revved his engine.

Suddenly he moved the gun away from my head and pressed it against my abdomen. Then he said something very ominous. I remember wondering whether what he said was directed at me, at the world in general, or to himself. It was one of those mysterious statements that could mean many things. I remember discussing it with people soon afterwards, debating who he was talking to and what he meant.

The fascinating thing is, when I try and recall those words now, I can't. I believe my mind has shut out that entire experience, to protect me from reliving too vividly what happened next. . . .

He pulled the trigger.

It wasn't like TV. The noise was deafening, especially at that time, reverberating off my apartment building and echoing out across the neighborhood. I clutched my stomach as I fell backwards onto the street. Then time slowed down to Matrix speed . . .

I calmly watched the shooter get into the car, which drove off towards Miami. I remember thinking for a second that I'd been had, that the gun must have been a starter pistol or shooting blanks, because I didn't feel anything. But when I looked down to where I was holding my abdomen, I saw blood streaming through my fingers.

Then I felt the pain. A lot.

As a writer and professional speaker, I pride myself on my ability to communicate ideas, concepts, and stories. But I simply don't have the words to adequately describe to you what a bullet tearing through vital organs feels like. We're talking white-hot, searing, thermonuclear hurt.

Because the shot was so loud, I expected lights would flash on, people would lean out windows, open doors, and then someone would come out and take care of me.

None of the above. Complete stillness.

I sat in the street, my legs splayed out under the streetlight. I remained there for who knows how long, suffering from shock, locked in a surreal, detached state, as I watched the pool of blood surrounding me grow larger. Suddenly I realized that if I didn't get up, go to my apartment, and call for help, I would die in the street.

I ripped off my shirt and tied it around me to stop the bleeding as best I could. I struggled up, crossed the street, climbed a flight of stairs, and entered my apartment. I managed to dial 911, then collapsed into a chair. I felt my life slowly ebbing away from me, as more and more of my blood flowed down onto the carpet.

By the time the paramedics arrived, I was so weak they picked up the chair with me in it and carried me down to the ambulance. When they lifted me onto the gurney, I writhed in pain as blood gushed from my gut. On the way to the hospital my blood pressure dropped so low they had to put me in a pressurized space suit to keep my heart pumping.

Once we arrived, emergency nurses greeted me with four IVs and a catheter. The doctors rushed me into surgery and sewed up my large intestine. My life had been saved, but I had yet to go through the worst agony I would ever experience . . .

For the next few days I could neither eat nor drink. They gave me a cotton swab to moisten my lips. A tube running through my nose, down my throat and into my stomach kept gagging me. Even through the fog of drugs, the pain was excruciating. When I choked on my own mucus and vomit, I ripped the tube out, only to have them reinstall it and threaten to strap my arms to the bedrails if I tried to remove it again.

The operations and recovery that followed made the next several months the most excruciatingly painful period of my life. The sutures ripped out of my stomach and infection set in. I couldn't find any comfortable way to sit, stand, or lie down. Two years passed before I felt normal again. What I endured I wouldn't wish on my worst enemy.

Yet imagine my shock when I realized later that I had subconsciously wished it all on myself.

Now, if you had told me this at the time, I no doubt would have slapped you into next week. But as you'll soon discover, I had indeed subconsciously attracted the whole painful experience. I was unknowingly following a pattern of victimhood that had been programmed into my subconscious mind since childhood. I was a helpless pawn, blindly manipulated by forces greater than I—just as you, too, probably have unknowingly manifested challenges for yourself, subconsciously attracted adversity, and even sabotaged your own success.

Now why would I do this? And why would you?

Later I'll explain the bizarre and robotic series of actions that caused me to bring such misfortune, suffering, and pain on myself. But first, let's explore whether you are being manipulated by these same forces—and might be sabotaging your own success and settling for less than you deserve in life.

And by *forces* I don't mean the usual suspects: the devil, terrorists, or communist insurgents. I'm not suggesting a *Da Vinci Code* conspiracy, nor am I reserving a seat on the next comet out. I'm talking about common, ever-present, and well-regarded people and institutions all around you right now, such as your family, your social circle, the place you worship, your government, and the media.

Because herein lies the real danger. If you are like most people, you think these institutions are part of your support network and working for your highest good. What you probably don't realize is that instead, *they are actually keeping you dumb, sick, and broke.*

It's not that your family doesn't love you or your friends don't like you. They probably do. And I doubt that your rabbi, minister, or priest consciously wants to cause you great harm. Your congressperson doesn't really have a vendetta against you, and the columnist in your daily newspaper isn't on a mission to harm you. At least not consciously.

But that won't stop all of these people, and thousands more, from causing you to subconsciously wreck your marriage, get passed over for promotions, manifest an illness or injury, sabotage your business, ingest substances that destroy your body, or do any one of a million other behaviors and actions that can prevent you from reaching the health, happiness, and prosperity that are your birthright.

I understand this may all sound crazy to you. Allow me to suggest the possibility that you have been so totally brainwashed with feelings of unworthiness, prejudice about wealth, and false beliefs about success, that you have unknowingly become your own worst enemy.

To find the cause, we have to go back to the formative years of your childhood—to look at the subconscious programming you were exposed to and the core beliefs that programming created. We must explore the world of *memes*, which are actually viruses of the mind.

Memes are like computer viruses in that they parasitize the host and cause it to replicate the memes. A hit song that you can't get out of your head is a meme, as is a catchy expression like "Just Do It!" Those are innocent enough memes. But there are many more memes that aren't so innocent.

Some of the memes you'll be exposed during the course of a week are likely to include "Buy furniture with no money down and no payments for two years," "If you drink our beer, you will be sexy and popular," and "When you buy our SUV, you'll be able to traverse fjords, climb mountains, and splash through rivers on your way to the dry cleaners."

Those endless chain e-mails that state, "Send this to everyone you know, and the people who care about you will send it back," "Help find this lost girl," and "Watch this amazing slide show of *Conversations with God*" are perfect examples of memes in action. When people receive these e-mails, they experience an emotional reaction and instantly feel compelled to forward them to everyone they know. (The term *meme* and the science of memetics were pioneered by Richard Dawkins in his book *The Selfish Gene*. And you'll learn much more about them in the book *Virus of the Mind* by Richard Brodie.)

The more emotion involved, the more likely a meme is to replicate. Of particular strength are memes involving children. (You'll see that demonstrated later in this chapter.) Case in point is all those new mothers who feel compelled to place "Baby on Board" decals in their car windows. What practical purpose could these signs actually achieve? Do they really think drivers in other cars are more cautious or slow down because they see one of these signs in the minivan window? But imagine the argument you would get from the mother of a newborn if you questioned this practice.

There is a whole group of memes that are interrelated (known as a *memeplex*) in the area of money and success. But these memes are about keeping you from achieving money and success, instead of helping you get it. They are very prevalent today, and a vast majority of the population is infected with them. These memes are readily accepted and replicated because they allow people to validate their lack of progress in their life goals. They include:

▌ Money is bad.
▌ Rich people are evil.

- It is spiritual or noble to be poor.
- If you struggle and grind it out, you'll be accepted by the rest of the nice people doing the same.
- Underdogs and the little guys are good; big entities are bad.
- You have to sell your soul to get rich.
- Rich people lie, cheat, and steal.
- CEOs, movie stars, and pro athletes are overpaid.
- Rich people have lots of money, but they also have many additional problems. Being rich isn't worth it.
- Money causes good people to go bad.
- If you deny yourself now, God will provide true prosperity in the afterlife.

It may be hard to believe that something a teacher or parent said when you were six years old is preventing you from getting a promotion today, but it could very well be so. You may doubt that a TV show you watched when you were 15 could be causing your marriage to suffer 20 years later, but that might be the case. You may find it far-fetched to think the books you read or the movies you enjoy could be causing you to stay sick or manifest disease.

But in fact, this is exactly what is happening to millions of people. And most likely you are one of them. As you are exposed to these people, institutions, and environments, you are likely to be infected by thousands of potential memes. Just as exposure to raw sewage can cause you to be infected with germs, microbes, and other nasty things, prolonged exposure to the *data-sphere* (meaning TV, radio, movies, books, magazines, newspapers, the Internet, and e-mail) will infect you with many nasty viruses of your mind.

Memes are as real—and deadly—as biological viruses. Just like computer viruses, memes parasitize the host (your mind), replicate, and spread to others. And just like other viruses, an epidemic of memes is sweeping through our society today.

Society spends billions to protect us from biological and computer viruses. Yet most people have never even heard of a mind virus. And they may be the most dangerous of all, because you don't realize you've been exposed to and then infected with them.

Obviously one of the big culprits is the data-sphere. All of these information and entertainment sources come with a slant—a bias, an opinion, or a point of view.

The obvious ones are not so much a problem. You probably listen to or watch a political commentator who you know is a rabid right-winger or bleeding-heart liberal. You know going in that Rush Limbaugh and Bill O'Reilly have a conservative bias, and that Howard Stern and Al Franken have a liberal one. That's not our concern.

The real danger is the insidious *subliminal* and *subconscious* programming you are getting—programming that is imprinted in your subconscious mind without your knowledge.

Let me give you an example. Suppose you're eight years old and your family drives by a mansion. You're impressed and say something about it. Your mother tells you that people who live in big houses like that aren't happy. The odds are quite good that you will be infected with the "money doesn't buy happiness" mind virus without even knowing it. It stays on your hard drive the rest of your life, but you don't even know the program was installed.

What's truly scary is that 90 percent of the programming you're exposed to today is the negative programming of lack, fear, and limitation. This programming causes you to self-sabotage your success and repel health and happiness. And it gets reinforced almost every time you watch TV, go to the movies, read a book, or have any connection with the data-sphere.

How Blockbuster Movies
Keep You Broke . . .

You probably saw the movie *Titanic*. If not, you're one of the last people on earth who hasn't. In fact, as of this writing, that movie is the highest grossing film ever released.

Why? Because it panders to the fear-based, lack-centered, and limiting beliefs that most people have about money and success. *Titanic* programs you on many different levels that it is noble to be poor, rich people are immoral, and money is evil. And the more you liked that movie, the more subconscious lack programming you have. I think it's the most evil movie ever made.

"Come on, Gage," you say. "It's just a love story. And it's a movie! We know it isn't real." But let's go to the movies the way *I* go to the movies . . .

The first scene of the movie opens with happy-go-lucky Jack. Now why is he happy-go-lucky? Because he's poor. He's only on the cruise because he won the trip in a card game, right?

So the first lesson we learn is that poor people are carefree and untroubled. Just think about all the problems rich people have. What if the butler calls in sick? What if somebody keys the Rolls? Have you seen the high cost of helicopter maintenance these days?

In scene two, we meet Rose. Now Rose is decidedly *not* happy. Why? Because she has to marry the boring rich guy. If you remember, her mother admonishes her to suck it up and go through with the wedding for the sake of the family. So the second lesson we learn (subconsciously, of course) is that you have to sell your soul and trade happiness for money.

As the movie develops, another critical scene shows Rose eating in the first class dining room. She is surrounded by all these dreary, stuffy, rich people who are sipping brandy, smoking cigars, and blathering inanely about polo matches and superficial nonsense. There's a shot with a mother slapping her little girl's wrist because she doesn't know how to use the eleventh oyster fork on the left. (Okay, I'm exaggerating. A little.)

Jack comes along and tells Rose, "Come on down to third class, and let me show you how to party!" Next, the movie cuts away to the poor people, who of course are singing, dancing, and having fun, showing us how much nicer and more fun they are to be around than those ponderous, nasty, and rigid rich people.

What's the subconscious programming here? Rich people are no fun. Poor people are the ones you want to hang out with. And if you want to be accepted and fit in with the crowd (something most people strive for all their lives, beginning in childhood), then you most certainly are better off being a poor person.

Then the ship hits the iceberg . . .

Rich people try to sneak into lifeboats or bribe their way on. Rose's wealthy fiancé even snatches a baby from its mother's arms in an effort to catch a ride. (Remember that memes involving emotion and children are particularly strong. So can you imagine the subconscious reaction imprinted upon your mind as you watch some selfish rich guy steal a baby from its mother to save his own skin?)

We see the rich people rowing into the horizon, as the water gurgles over the poor bastards chained up in the lower decks. We see a brave, poor mother as she calmly tells her children that they are going to go downstairs and sing church hymns until they drown. Excuse me while I puke!

Fast-forward to the end of the movie. Rose is now about 180 years old. Her poor granddaughter is working her fingers to the bone, taking care of this old bag. Rose has a necklace worth about $40 million, which she could give to her granddaughter and set her up for life. What does she do with it?

She feeds it to the friggin' sharks!

Level, after level, after level, this movie subconsciously programs you that money is bad, rich people are evil, and it is good, even spiritual, to be poor. And nothing could be further from the truth.

"Okay, I'll give you that one," you say. "But that's just one movie."

Just one movie? Well, let's look at a few more blockbusters. Take *Spiderman*, for example. In the first *Spiderman*, who was the dastardly villain? The billionaire rich guy. By the way, who was the villain in *The Fantastic Four*, *Alien*, and almost every James Bond movie ever made? The rich guy. But back to our web-weaving crusader.

Remember when poor Peter Parker finally met up with the girl next door whom he had secretly worshipped from afar for years? They each go to throw the garbage out at the same time. Their eyes meet. She begins talking to Peter, and the sparks start flying. Then what happens?

The rich kid pulls up in his brand new car, which his evil, rich daddy just bought him for his birthday. The girl shrieks with delight, drops Peter along with the garbage, hops into the car, and they drive off, leaving Peter scorned, dejected, and alone. On a subconscious level, how do you think that makes you feel about rich people?

There's even a part in the movie when Peter's uncle says the most famous lack-programming words ever spoken:

"We may not be rich, but at least we're honest."

Ever heard anything like that? What does that really mean? Let me translate: "Be glad you are poor. That means you are honest, noble, and a good person—because rich people lie, cheat, and steal."

That's why something you may have heard from a parent or teacher when you were 10 could be impacting your core beliefs 20, 30, even 40 years later. When you are young and impressionable, things you hear from people in authority create an indelible effect on you.

Now why was Peter's uncle raising him? Because he was an orphan. Remember, memes are strongest when they are emotional and involve children. What could grab your heart more than a poor little orphan? So Spiderman was an orphan. Come to think of it, so was Batman. And Superman. Wonder Woman. Harry Potter. The Boxcar Children and the Lemony Snicket kids are all orphans.

Do you detect a pattern here?

You may be starting to wonder whether this is a conspiracy among writers to manipulate you. It isn't. They are infected with the same memes and don't even know they are replicating them.

Like the original, *Spiderman II* was riddled with subliminal programming to reinforce negative mind viruses. Which, coincidentally, ensured it would be another smash hit worldwide. Once again, we meet Peter's noble aunt who raised him. We can tell she's noble, because the greedy bankers are evicting her from her house.

In the sequel, Peter loses his pizza delivery job, because he stopped to save two little kids who were about to be run over by a truck. This reinforces the meme that noble people sacrifice their own good and happiness for others (which will create more negative and dysfunctional relationships, because we certainly don't have enough of those around!). Then to make it just perfect, the heartless boss is an East Indian, reinforcing the meme that those money-grubbing immigrants are here stealing all the good jobs from hard-working Americans.

Of course, *Spiderman I* ends with our hero telling his one true love that he could never be with her. Then he walks off alone into the sunset of his unrequited love. He has made the choice to give away his own happiness so he can serve others and fight the forces of evil.

In *Spiderman II*, the girl gets pushier, pressing Peter to make her an honest woman. Again Peter is conflicted between pursuing his own happiness or wrapping thugs in spider webs. So he asks his aunt (who is now sorting her possessions on the street) what to do. She tells him that there are special people in the world, people who sacrifice everything that is important to them to serve others for the greater good. Is that sweet or what?

What a crock of spider shit!

Hollywood, Bollywood, Hong Kong, and movie makers everywhere have learned the lesson well. The more a movie conforms to your beliefs, the more certain you are to like it. Of course, it's not just the movie studios . . .

Television is just as guilty—and a lot more dangerous to your health, happiness, and prosperity, because you are probably exposed to TV more than any other media.

Think about how millionaires and billionaires are portrayed on the small screen. The entire premise of shows like *The Beverly Hill-billies* is that rich people are snobby, pretentious buffoons, and poor people are kind-hearted, good folk with common sense. Remember the goofy millionaire with the pretentious name on *Gilligan's Island*? Wasn't there always one rich guy in the tent on *MASH* who listened to opera, acted like a jerk, and generally made life difficult for the good ole' boys? Think back to the way those adulterous, lying, cheating, and conniving rich people were portrayed on *Dallas*, *Dynasty*, and similar shows. Instant replay, the same tune is played over and over.

But from a prosperity standpoint, probably the most insidious shows came when networks discovered how cheaply reality shows could be produced—and how popular they would become. Shows like *Survivor, Fear Factor, The Apprentice,* and *Weakest Link* share a common thread: how much people will demean themselves to get on TV and try for a cash prize. (Of course, a similar dynamic can be found with the *Jerry Springer Show* and the other daytime talk trash-a-thons.)

The latest hit as of this writing is *Unanimous.* It pits nine people in a bunker, each one scheming how to go home with $1.5 million and let the other eight leave empty-handed. Of course, the producers seeded the group with a couple of liars and cheats, to reinforce your belief that money causes people to do bad things.

You cannot watch shows such as these without lowering your opinion and expectation of humanity. You lose respect for your fellow human beings, and, as a result, lose respect for *yourself.*

Which takes us right back to the worthiness issue. If you don't think you're worthy, you will always end up sabotaging your happiness—whether that means enjoying good health, building strong relationships, making money, or achieving professional success. In developed countries (and I use that term loosely), people are watching five to six hours of television a day! Can you imagine what that does to a person's self-esteem over a period of years?

Take any decade going back to the birth of TV and I can tell you which television programs were successful because they pandered to widely accepted beliefs that money is bad, rich people are evil, or it is inherently spiritual to be poor.

Unfortunately books, magazines, and newspapers continue the negative programming of their electronic counterparts. Think about this: How many books have you read where the guy gives up everything to get the girl? Or books that play out the same scenarios as the TV and movie scripts I've described, where rich people are evil and poor people are spiritual?

Flying over to Europe a few years ago, I happened to read an advance write-up about a then soon-to-be-released book, *The Nanny Diaries*. It was a collection of anecdotes from two nannies about how vapid, shallow, and conniving their rich clients were. They talked about the wealthy woman who was too busy alphabetizing her lingerie drawers to take care of her kids, and a negligent father and his "thong-sporting mistress." I immediately predicted in my newsletter that this book would become a smash bestseller, which of course it did.

Poor people love to read anything that depicts rich people as unhappy, superficial, or dishonest. Then they can tell themselves that the real reason they aren't rich is because they aren't willing to lower themselves to become like that. (Just like the mother who tells her kids as they drive by the rich houses that those people can't possibly be happy.)

I remember reading a John Grisham novel about a lawyer from a big downtown law firm who meets a homeless person. The lawyer quits his job and goes to work at a law clinic for street people. Along the way, he divorces his wife, sells his Lexus to buy an old beater, and moves into a dumpy apartment with no heat and furniture so he can be like his clients.

How romantic. How stupid.

Of course, this book also became a monster bestseller. But how many people could that lawyer have helped if he had stayed at his $200,000-a-year job at the big firm? What if he got the partners to each agree to work half a day a month for free in the law clinic? What if he went to the other members of the bar association in his hometown and got them to do the same thing? Those homeless people would have more lawyers than they'd know what to do with!

But you will never see that book, because it would never get published. No one wants to hear about rich people staying rich and helping others. We want to hear that money and what it can buy aren't important. We want to read that someone "gave it all away for love."

Think of the many songs, plays, and operas that parallel those exact themes. There's a sappy country love song with the lyrics, "He owns half of downtown Atlanta; all I can give her is the moon." Of course, this is just the kind of pap that makes a hit, because it panders to the lack programming that the masses have.

The irony of all this is that the people who sell you this stuff get very rich. Grisham is now one of the wealthiest authors in the world. Alan Jackson makes millions singing country ditties about "the little man." James Cameron made about $200 million from *Titanic*, teaching you that it is spiritual to be poor!

Now, again, it's not that there's an organized conspiracy to keep you broke. The people involved in spreading these memes usually don't even know what they're doing. Musicians get influenced by what was successful in the past. Screenwriters look back at classics to see what was popular. Television writers just regurgitate old concepts again and again. The cycle of programming repeats, and the resulting beliefs are embedded in society.

But we haven't even got to the worst part, the most dangerous part of the whole programming equation: the victimhood and entitlement mentality it creates in you.

One reason these writers keep repeating the cycle is because they rely on timeless themes or archetypes—some of which have been around for hundreds, even thousands of years. The most prevalent of these is the "hero's journey." They teach this in Writing 101. The basic premise of this theme is an ordinary person who is presented with a difficult challenge and shows extraordinary courage and resourcefulness to overcome it and emerge victorious.

Star Wars is a hero's journey, as are *Spiderman, Batman, Lord of the Rings,* all Robert Ludlum novels, and just about every action movie and spaghetti western ever made. We identify with the hero and want to become him or her. Which is how I ended up getting shot on that Saturday night. Quite simply, I manifested it.

It all started many years ago in my childhood. I wasn't happy as a kid, and never fit in. I didn't seem to belong in my family, couldn't relate to the other kids in school, and never felt comfortable anyplace else. I spent hours upon hours alone in my room, reading books.

I spent most of that time fantasizing about escaping my miserable existence and living my own hero's journey. I think most kids do this; depressed kids just do it a lot more. Books, and to a lesser extent, movies, and television were my escape.

As formulaic and predictable as book, TV, and movie adventures have become, one premise played out time and again. The hero gets shot. He will suffer, gut it out, and ultimately live. (The shot usually just grazed the arm, so he got all of the attention, was bandaged up, and ended up looking cool, without having to worry about the irritating stuff like dying. Unless of course he was that *extra* crew member who beamed down to the planet with Captain Kirk, Mr. Spock, Sulu, and Bones!)

Every time John Wayne got shot, I imagined the sympathy people would be feeling for me when I got shot. I lived out that fantasy a million times in my youth. Then I grew up and lived it out as a reality.

So I really believe that I manifested getting shot on that street corner. Just like I manifest everything that happens in my life, both the good and the bad. *Just like you attract and manifest everything that happens to you.*

It is the law of attraction. We attract what we think about—that which we lust after, and that which we fear. Anything that consumes our thoughts gets manifested in the real world.

The skeptics scoff at such a premise. How would my assailant know I subconsciously longed to be shot to facilitate my hero's journey fantasy? What made him pick that street on that night to find someone to rob?

I don't know. But I do know this: Joseph Campbell talks about the collective unconscious. Einstein spoke of the unified field, and Vedic sages speak of the space between thoughts. We know that at its ultimate level, everything (including people, elevators, oceans, guns, and trees) is an energy vibration. So while I can't tell you exactly *how* the law of attraction works, I can tell you it does.

Another timeless theme is unrequited love. You can look back at *Romeo and Juliet*; when Mimi dies, leaving Rodolfo alone in La Boheme; or when Tosca cries to Scarpia to meet her before God, then leaps to her death, in the opera bearing her name. It is the unrequited love meme, over and over.

Remember the TV show *The Incredible Hulk*? Every week Dr. David Banner travels to a new town, meets a beautiful woman, and falls in love. Then something happens to anger him and he "Hulks out." He has to flee town before the tabloid reporter catches up with him. Every single show ends the same way: with him hitchhiking his way out of town, alone, as the piano music plays. . . .

Fast-forward to today and you have Spiderman walking away from his love at the end of the first movie, or *Crouching Tiger, Hidden Dragon,* and *House of the Flying Daggers*, which are just reworks of *Romeo and Juliet*. They all get their emotional hook (which is critical

21

for influencing and programming your subconscious mind) from this timeless and universal theme of unrequited love.

The big breakout hit for 2005 was the medical drama *House*. Actually, the acting is quite good, and I enjoy the show. But the real reason it's a smash hit is because it panders to some very strong memes. Dr. House is a maverick and a wise guy, always flouting authority. (Meme: Root for the little guy fighting the forces of evil.) The subplot of season one was the greedy billionaire who took over as chairman of the board and wanted to fire people, generate more sales for his pharmaceutical company, and run the hospital as a profit center. He didn't care if sick people died, because there wasn't enough money to be made by saving them. (Meme: Rich people are evil.)

The subplot for the second season had House reuniting with his ex and discovering they both still loved each other. Then House pushed her aside so she could go back to her sickly new husband. (Meme: Unrequited love.) The same note, over and over.

How Government Discourages Success . . .

As I told you up front, the media is just one of the guilty parties. There are plenty of other entities working nonstop to program you with memes of lack and limitation. You can start with your government. Obviously, if you live in a communist or socialist country, the government needs to program you to believe wealth is bad, citizens are responsible for taking care of everybody else, and it is everyone's sacred duty to sacrifice their own happiness for the collective.

The real danger is in places like the United States, the United Kingdom, France, Australia, Canada, and dozens of other countries that claim to be democracies or republics operating under the free-enterprise system. They talk a good game of free-market economies, but their affirmative action programs, antimonopoly witch hunts, and socialized medical care actually circumvent innovation, low prices, and value-for-value exchange.

By their very nature, governments are corrupt. Either they are headed by fascist dictator types, where the evil is apparent, or they present themselves as governments for the people, and the evil is hidden. The governments operating as loose democracies eventually work their way into a two-party system. Then each party must compete with the other for power, with their success based on their ability to give away more pork than the other party. If party A offers free high school, party B has to up the ante with free college. If party A offers free prescriptions for senior citizens, party B needs to trump that with national health care. Political parties retain or reclaim power by promising the population more perks than they take in through taxes.

But, of course, the only free cheese is in the mousetrap. The only way to provide all this largesse is to take it away from the smaller percentage of wealthy voters and distribute it among the larger group of broke voters (who believe they are innocent victims of the system, and think it's only righteous that they are given some of the spoils of those greedy rich people).

The most dangerous individual to a government is a wealthy, sophisticated person who can take care of his or her own needs. The perfect citizen for a government is a needy one, because the more you need the government, the more controllable you are.

As a creative, thinking human being, you are up against a mass of people who want something for nothing and governments around the world who want to give it to them. The sad truth is that your government doesn't want you to be successful. It wants and needs you to be a worker drone in the collective to support its system of dispensing free cheese to maintain its power structure. So you can be sure every interaction with the government will foster programming to support this.

Religion . . .

Your religion probably doesn't want you to be successful either. Healthy, happy, self-sustained people don't need much guidance and support. You're a lot easier to manipulate and control (and compel into kicking into the collection basket) if you're praying for deliverance, salvation, or a new job.

Organized religion probably promotes more harmful memes that hold back more people than any other entity. For this reason, I devote an entire chapter to the devastating and debilitating effect organized religion has on millions of people around the world.

There is another, extremely dangerous source of programming, constantly assaulting you, yet one that few people realize . . .

The People You Spend Time With . . .

Nothing will infect you with a negative view of the world faster than hanging around people with harmful belief systems. And it's even worse when you are trying to "save" a bunch of them. Because the harder you try to pull them up, the more they are subconsciously trying to pull you down. Some of this will be intentional; most of it won't be. But that unintentional programming is the most deadly.

That's not to say that your family and friends don't mean well; I'm sure that, in their own way, most of them do. Parents teach their kids to go for the secure jobs, maybe even get union wages if they're lucky. Teachers and guidance counselors tell you to "be realistic." Friends tell you not to strive for too much, lest you be disappointed.

Most of this they will do subconsciously, out of fear you will get too successful and leave them behind. Then, of course, there are those friends and family who truly don't want you to be rich and successful—because if you get healthy, wealthy, and happy, they lose their excuses about why it isn't possible for them.

They will explain how foolish your business idea is, ridicule your dreams, and disparage your goals. And if you retreat back to mediocrity, they will placate you and validate your lack of success with the usual platitudes, such as, "You have to have money to make money," "You have to sell your soul to be rich," and "You need the right connections to be successful."

There are certain people in your life who are toxic. Spending time with them is dangerous for your hopes, aspirations, and dreams. They infect your mind with fear, doubt, and uncertainty. When you are just coming out of negative beliefs and programming, you are very weak and susceptible to backsliding. Often you will need to keep physical and emotional distance between you and your old contacts for a certain period of time.

I have people I love, and would love to help. But I recognize that they are not really ready to be helped right now. And spending a great deal of time with them is dangerous to my own emotional well-being.

Now, I am pretty developed, and quite strong, so I can withstand a lot. I can spend time with people at lower consciousness and help bring them up, instead of them bringing me down. But that's because I have been on this path for 15 years. There was a time when the opposite would have happened. And still today, I stay away from certain environments, because the number of negative, victim-mentality people is so large that I fear it will infect my consciousness. You have to do the same.

If you are just starting to break out of lack and move toward prosperity, you must be extra vigilant about this. The most important resources you will ever have are your mind and your mind-set. You must protect them at all costs.

Jim Rohn tells us that your income will be the average earnings of your five closest friends. I think this holds true for the quality of your marriage or relationship, your health, and every other area of prosperity.

So How Does All This Play Out?

You become exposed to the data-sphere as you grow up. Your friends and family slowly chip away at your dreams and self-esteem. Maybe you join an organized religion that teaches you that you were born a sorry sinner.

Little by little, in subtle ways, you get programmed. You create beliefs that get cemented in your personality. You don't realize you are doing this, but you are. Your core, foundational beliefs about relationships, money, and success will all be programmed into you *by the time you are 10 years old.*

Once you are programmed for lack and limitation, you instinctively start to gravitate to the downtrodden, the poor, and the underdogs. You begin to distrust wealthy people. Your self-esteem drops and you develop worthiness issues. Your dreams get smaller; they seem more distant and less attainable. (And remember, all of this is happening subconsciously.) If your self-esteem gets low enough, you'll do as I did: You'll create a more dramatic hero's journey for yourself, to attempt to feel better about yourself.

You will subconsciously and unknowingly create obstacles, challenges, and setbacks for everything you try to do. You will take projects and accomplishments that would actually be simple for you and make them more difficult to give you a more heroic story. The more drama, the more trauma—and the more noble, brave, and heroic it will make you feel. Or at least that's the idea. Of course, it never works out that way, because you just keep setting the target farther and farther away, so you're determined to fail and feel even worse about yourself.

I ought to know. I did that for 30 years.

I was a teenage alcoholic and drug addict. I went to jail for armed robbery when I was just 15. After straightening myself out, I successfully failed at no less than 10 different business ventures. I attracted 11 negative relationships in a row. It all culminated when I turned 30 and the IRS seized my business for nonpayment of taxes and auctioned it off at the courthouse.

After this last event, I had no house, no car, no job, and was $55,000 in debt. I sold my furniture to pay the rent and ate macaroni and cheese three times a day. Finally I had to ask myself the most important question: *Was there one person who was always at the scene of the crime?*

Of course, I didn't like the answer—but it was the answer I needed, because it got me to stop looking at outside factors and instead look within. I began a study of prosperity which has continued to this day. And I began a path of self-development and personal growth. Along the way, I came to realize that I had been sabotaging my own success for 30 years, because I didn't think I was worthy.

So what about you? Do you think you have been influenced by all of the lack and limitation programming you've been exposed to? Is it possible you have subconsciously been sabotaging your success and rejecting wealth, health, and happiness because you are hanging on to beliefs that don't serve you? Who are the five people you spend the most time with? What kind of programming are you getting from them?

The Conflict . . .

What all this subconscious programming sets up is a below-the-surface conflict in your mind. Your rational, logical, conscious mind tells you that you want to be healthy, happy, and prosperous. Let's face it, who wouldn't?

So you think you want to be rich. But your subconscious mind tells you that rich people lie, cheat, and steal. Your core foundational belief is that these people have to sell their soul to get rich. Your subconscious mind reminds you that you want to be well-liked, to be a person of integrity, and to go to heaven when you die.

So you pass up a great opportunity, do something to get fired, turn to drugs or alcohol addiction, mess up your marriage, or experience just enough self-doubt that you back down and quit at the first sign of adversity. You give up on your dreams and resolve to be more "realistic."

The biggest casualty is your self-esteem. Most five-year-olds have good self-esteem. By the time those five-year-olds get to college age, most of them will have self-esteem programmed out of them. Now you begin to question if you are worthy of health, happiness, and wealth.

Once you have worthiness issues, you'll never let yourself achieve happiness. And no one does more to program people that they are not worthy than organized religion. Which is where we will explore next.

CHAPTER 2

Hope, Dope, and the Pope: The Battle for Control of Your Spirit

■ ■ ■

**Cosmic Frequent Flyer Programs
and Other Religious Beliefs That Cause You
to Sabotage Your Success and Happiness**

■ ■ ■

happened to be overseas when the late Pope John Paul II died. I thought the United States was wrapped up in the funeral rituals, but in Europe, the media fixation made the coverage in the States look positively skimpy. In Paris, French TV might as well have been billed as "all Pope, all the time." When I went to Amsterdam, even the hashish coffee shops had their TVs tuned into the spectacle nonstop.

In his 26-year papacy, Pope John Paul II touched the world like none before him. He introduced computers into the Vatican, traveled to 129 countries, and harnessed the power of television and technology to reach every corner of the globe. He used his visits to shake up right wing dictatorships, give hope to the poor, and shine a spotlight on the afflicted. By all accounts, he was a well-meaning and deeply committed man.

None of that will change the legacy of poverty, ignorance, and despair he left behind for his followers . . .

As history has demonstrated time and again, it is not the evil villains we need fear most, but rather the well-meaning crusaders. And John Paul II was certainly a crusader. He worked to overthrow communism, comfort the sick, and nurture the poor. Yet like most religious leaders, his actions actually worked to keep his followers dumb, sick, and broke.

Now don't get me wrong: I don't think he did this because he was an evil man. He impressed me as a very spiritual and caring human being. A human being infected with so many common memes, he had no idea of the desolation he was creating.

The Pope fought communism in his native Poland and around the globe. But he was still infected with the communistic belief that it is noble to be poor, and money is evil. He came to the United States seven times, and each time he denounced American materialism, castigating Americans for not sharing more of their wealth with the world's poor. In fact, he scorned the effects of capitalism at every opportunity—except when the collection basket made the rounds.

We've looked hard at the lack and limitation beliefs that people get programmed with from the data-sphere and their social circle. But historically, no one has used negative programming better than organized religion. And of course the Vatican is usually near the top of the list.

You already know what I think about the subliminal messages of most blockbuster movies. Naturally, when *The Passion of the Christ* took off at the box office, I couldn't help but assume it must be riddled with lack programming. I bought some popcorn and went to see for myself. Halfway through the movie I had seen enough to prove my case.

What a depressing movie! And what a perfect film to pander to the millions of Christians who are completely brainwashed with the notion that they are sorry sinners, flawed beings needing redemption, and not worthy of the grace their beloved Savior offers them. Give Mel Gibson credit: He sure knows how to target the perfect market demographic. And casting Jesus as a white guy—what a brilliant stroke of marketing savvy!

You know that with every snap of the whip that slashed Jesus' flesh and splattered his blood, every Christian watching felt guiltier and guiltier. Every time he fell with that heavy cross and picked it up again, every viewer knew they were more unworthy. And when the soldiers started driving the spikes through his hands and feet, Christian viewers felt the anguish of knowing they could never meet the standard, no matter how many rosary beads they rubbed, how many Hail Mary's they chanted, or how meek they could become.

And just as they lined up to see their Savior whipped and crucified in the Gibson movie, millions lined up in Rome for the Pope's funeral to assuage their guilt by feeling guiltier. For many Catholics, the more unworthy they feel, the better they think their chances are for salvation. In reality, all this does is lower their self-esteem, exacerbate their worthiness issues, and increase their self-sabotage behavior here on earth.

Of all the people I have coached in removing their prosperity blocks, those with unworthiness issues created by religion are the hardest ones to bust. That's because religion is so emotional for most people, and core religious beliefs are usually hard-wired by the time you are five or six years old.

The spectacle around the death of the Pope and the coronation of Pope Benedict XVI embedded this message deeper and deeper. Normally I don't read anything in the newspaper other than the baseball news. But the front page, four-color spread on the Pope's passing sucked me in.

Even in death, the mind viruses started by John Paul II carried forward, continuing to infect people with a fear-based existence. The article on the front page of *The Miami Herald* said, "But when he died Saturday night in his Vatican apartment at age 84, it was his very public pain and suffering that marked the last decade of his papacy—his way of reminding his flock that redemption comes through suffering."

A little later it added, "Everything he did in his papacy—the third longest in history—stemmed from his unshakable belief that only faith, forged in the crucible of suffering, could fulfill God's designs for human beings."

Of course, this is just the perpetuation of the "You're a sorry sinner and if you suffer and sacrifice enough, we might make an exception for you and let you at the good stuff in the afterlife" dogma that organized religion has been brainwashing people with for centuries. (And notice how the newspaper writer is unknowingly a carrier of the virus, continuing to spread it to hundreds of thousands more people.)

In almost every pronouncement or appearance he made, the Pope did much to perpetuate this belief that you must suffer now if you want to get the good stuff later. He once told his biographer, "I have to lead Christ's church into the third millennium by prayer. But I saw that this is not going to be enough. She must be led by suffering. By sacrifice."

Sheesh! Now *I'm* feeling guilty, beginning to worry that I may be struck down by a lightning bolt for that Cinnabon I ate in the airport.

Pope John Paul II reached out to Jews, Muslims, Protestants, and people of other faiths—while never missing a chance to let them know that the one door to salvation was going to be slammed in their face in the moment of truth. He was forceful in his rejection of homosexuality, birth control, divorce, remarrying after divorce, and women and married men in the clergy. And because he appointed 95 percent of the cardinals who chose his successor, his rigid orthodox theological vision will likely be imprinted on the Church for many more decades to come.

Right now, another generation of kids in Sunday schools and private Christian schools are becoming infected with self-loathing, guilt, and worthiness issues as the church marches on. More gay teens will take their lives, believing they have been forsaken by their God. More women will receive the message that they are second-class citizens. More people will stay in marriages they never should have been in, living their entire lives in dismal resignation.

And let's not just single out the Vatican. It may be Suffering Central, but plenty of franchises abound in our culture. The same horrific manipulation of young minds is happening in many temples, mosques, and synagogues around the world. Millions more children are right now receiving the same negative programming that will relegate them to lives of suffering, limitation, and fear.

And what a despicable, tragic, and heinous crime that is.

The real problem stems from the fundamentalists in organized religions. They have hijacked the true message and distorted it to reflect their agenda. These are not unknowing victims, manipulated by mind viruses. These are cold, calculated people, who use memes to manipulate their followers to strengthen their power base. Hateful bigots like Pat Robertson, Jerry Falwell, and Oral Roberts claim to teach the lessons of the Bible. Murderers like Osama bin Laden profess to represent true Islam. But they are simply conniving zealots, twisting the true message of their faith to unduly influence the faithful.

A few years ago, the press reported the Arab world was outraged because Israeli soldiers had killed Islamic cleric Sheik Ahmed Yassin, the spiritual leader of Hamas. What kind of world do we live in when a person can get a job running an organization that recruits and trains assassination squads and suicide bombers, yet still be called a "cleric" or a "spiritual leader"?

Fundamentalism has evolved into a code word for hate, persecution, and intolerance. Idiots like Robertson, Falwell, and Roberts no more teach the message of Jesus Christ than bin Laden, Yassin, and Saddam Hussein represent the true message of Islam. They have simply manipulated the message and used it to program their mindless followers.

In Chapter 1 we explored the phenomenon of the hero's journey. As kids, we grew up being profoundly affected by these heroic journey influences and fantasizing about one day becoming the hero ourselves. These fantasies could have been wanting to grow up and be tough like John Wayne or Bruce Willis, save the world like Buck Rogers and Luke Skywalker, or develop superhuman powers like Wonder Woman, Superman, and the Fantastic Four.

But then we grew up and found a world that didn't have a lot of job openings for superheroes. And who knew where to buy the cape and tights? So we created the next best thing: *our own hero's journey.* By developing an addiction we have to overcome. By getting in relationships with dysfunctional partners we must break free of. By creating business failures we must surmount. By manifesting illnesses that must be defeated. (Or, in my case, all of the above.)

You see, the more worthiness issues you have and the lower your self-esteem, the more heroic a journey you need to validate yourself! So you attract another abusive partner, switch to a new addiction, find another dead-end job, or manifest another tumor. Everyone who knows you confirms what a string of "bad luck" you have had. Everyone tells you that you're an inspiration. You feel noble, for all the sacrifice you've had to make.

There's only one problem with all this: Your life sucks.

But before you completely give up hope, organized religion rides in to the rescue. The proponents of this religion—priests, rabbis, and other holy people—assure you that you are meant to suffer here to demonstrate your worthiness for the afterlife, when you'll get all the real good stuff.

And, depending on the religion, if you prostrate yourself enough, beg for forgiveness enough, say enough "Hail Mary's," ambush enough American GIs, rub enough rosary beads, pray to Mecca enough times each day, blow up enough abortion clinics, kill enough Jews, or send enough money to the televangelist—you will be saved.

Most of the world's major organized religions are set up as cosmic frequent flier programs. If you collect enough points, you earn the free trip to paradise!

Whether we look at the Christian concept of original sin, the Buddhist eightfold path, the Hindu doctrine of karma, the Jewish Covenant, or the Muslim Code of Law, all of these religious concepts are set up with the basic presupposition that we are flawed beings who need salvation. And if that's what you are taught beginning at four or five years old, is it any wonder that you would grow up with worthiness issues, low self-esteem, fear-based consciousness, and a tendency to self-sabotage?

If you went to a private Catholic school and the nuns told you that you were born a sorry sinner, what are the odds you are going to grow up liking yourself? If you are a Hindu who believes that this time around you are reincarnated from an Egyptian horse thief to pay penance, what are the chances you're going let yourself be successful? If you're a Buddhist who believes you must go through 129 lifetimes to find enlightenment—and you're only on lifetime 57—what are the odds that you're going to let yourself become wealthy this time?

One of the best steps you can take to become healthy, happy, and rich is to do some serious critical thinking about your religious beliefs. Think about what subliminal messages come from those beliefs and what you were exposed to as a young child. You will find many clues in those memories as to what has caused you to create the results you have in your life right now.

And let's get this straight: I have studied all the major religions of the world extensively, and I believe their true message is one of love, not hate; of abundance, not lack. The lack-centered messages of hate, intolerance, and poverty are coming from the fundamentalists who have hijacked the messages to perpetuate their power base. The real message of these religions is love and abundance.

You are not serving God, the world, or yourself by playing small. I believe that poverty is a sin, and you are meant to be rich. Your assignment on this planet is to unfold into the true greatness you are capable of, and model that success to inspire others to escape the mediocrity their lives have become.

It's not all mental, however. We exist in the physical realm as well. And we each were issued a body in which to carry around our soul. And there is another set of forces—forces devoted to breaking down and harming your body and leading you into another form of subjugation. Let's look at that next . . .

CHAPTER 3

Junk Food Junkies: The Battle for Control of Your Body

■ ■ ■

The Conspiracy to Keep You Sick, Fat, and Lethargic

■ ■ ■

I sat by my 86-year-old grandfather's bedside as he lay in a hospital during his final days. He faded in and out of consciousness. When lucid, he told me point blank, "I'm not getting out of here. I don't want to."

This was no surprise to me. I remembered a couple years earlier when his sister (my great aunt, Nettie, also in her 80s) told me that the upcoming Christmas would be her last one. At that time, I tried to argue, pleading with her to not affirm such a negative statement. She shut me down fast:

"I don't *want* to live another year," she replied. "I'm too sick. I can't sleep. I am in pain all the time. I can't take it any more. I want to have this last Christmas, and then I'm done." And that is exactly what she did.

So when my grandfather told me he wanted to play his last hand, all I could do was love him and support the choice he made. I wanted him to hang around so I'd have someone to call on Father's Day, go to a Marlins game with, or just talk to about old times. But I couldn't ask him to endure any more pain and suffering. Like his sister, he had been in poor health for over a decade, and almost every moment of every day was a challenge.

When my grandmother reached her final days, she couldn't express such a sentiment. And I doubt she ever would have, being the type who never wanted to burden anyone. But we'll never know, because Alzheimer's disease stole her mind from us. However, she too experienced great suffering and pain in her final years.

Pretty much all of the aging folks in my family have shared two constants: the typical American diet, and the disease, breakdown, and suffering that are the result of it. Unfortunately, this is the diet America has exported around the world, along with the negative results.

No book on prosperity and success could be complete without looking at the wellness part of the equation. One could easily argue that health may be the most important component of an abundant lifestyle, yet it is an aspect most people ignore. In fact, people often trade away their health to get a particular job, win a promotion, or earn a certain amount of money. You learn quickly enough that it isn't worth it. Getting to your golden years with a sizable nest egg but without the good health to enjoy it is the cruelest irony.

Another issue is that people never achieve their dreams because they don't have the mental acuity, good health, or necessary energy or to realize those dreams. For years I stated that I would become rich if I could just get my body to keep up with my mind. And ultimately, that's what it took for me: getting my health to the level where I could operate at a peak state of performance. If you are like most people, your wellness is seriously lagging behind where you would like to be on the path of success.

The Battle for Control of Your Body

In the last 30 years, forward movement has been made in the areas of health and wellness at what most people consider an amazing rate. Cures for many diseases have been discovered, treatments to contain many other diseases developed, and huge strides made in nutrition. The end result of all of these advances has been that, while most people are living longer lives, they are assailed with health issues and disease and end up spending their final years in misery. There is an epidemic of high cholesterol, high blood pressure, heart attacks, diabetes, arthritis, Alzheimer's, and other degenerative diseases.

Where's does this universal breakdown in health come from? I believe it's the result of two ominous trends in the foods that we eat.

The first of these has been the steady *transformation of foods into addictive substances*. The potato chip company can have their catchy slogan of "Bet you can't eat just one," but that innocent catch phrase actually foreshadowed a serious and concerted effort to make foods addictive.

Creating foods that make you physically desire them again and again is very big business. So big, in fact, that the tobacco companies have slowly transitioned from trying to hook you on cigarettes to getting you to crave junk food instead. This business is even better than cigarettes, because most of the junkies don't know they are hooked. (For more insights on this, read *The Wellness Revolution* by Paul Zane Pilzer.)

Because of what we now know about smoking, a company like Philip Morris can no longer advertise and target youngsters to hook them on Marlboros. But they don't need to, because they have free rein to hook kids on goodies like Oreo Cookies, Cheez Whiz, Kool-Aid Slushies, Jell-O, Life Savers, and Ritz Crackers instead.

Today, millions of people have unknowingly become junk food

junkies because many of the foods we are being programmed to buy have a strong physiological addictive factor.

Let's look at how it works in layperson's terms. We all have bacteria in our digestive track. Most of us know we have good bacteria and bad bacteria. We need both. When in balance, the two bacteria create the perfect environment to digest our food, extract the necessary nutrients out of it, and eliminate the rest from our body as waste.

When we eat refined flour products (like white bread, crackers, pastries, chips, and pasta), they feed the bad bacteria in our colon. Foods with yeast in them do the same thing. Eating sugar also causes the bad bacteria to multiply rapidly. And, of course, the refined sugar we have in our diets today dramatically speeds that up. Making matters much worse, refined sugar is now added to practically everything you can consume (which is perfect for creating an addiction, as you soon will see).

Of course we know that sugary sweets like Krispy Kreme donuts, Cinnabons, cotton candy, ice cream, and soda are virtually all sugar. But did you also know that tomato ketchup, frozen peas, spaghetti sauce, salad dressings, and about a million other things contain sugar?

In any event, this refined sugar, yeast, and refined flour acts like fertilizer to the bad bacteria in your intestinal track, causing it to run amok. It actually makes you crave more yeast, refined flour, and sugary foods. So you lose the willpower to pass up dessert, continue to crave bread or rolls, and find yourself wanting another soda an hour after the first. It really is a physical addiction.

If you eat ice cream, cookies, or potato chips, you will keep craving more. And the more you eat, the stronger that physiological urge becomes. This keeps feeding the bad bacteria in your digestive track, which increases your physical cravings to eat yet more.

As this bad bacteria runs amok, you lose the natural peristaltic action that moves food through your colon and on to final elimination. Instead you become impacted, with your last meal pushing through the rancid, decaying, and putrefying previous meals. These toxins in your digestive track seep back into your blood stream, and there is increasing evidence that this autotoxicity is responsible for many modern-day ailments, such as chronic fatigue syndrome, lethargy, hyperactivity, and even Attention Deficit Disorder. In addition, your colon walls become encrusted, reducing your ability to receive nutrients from the food you eat. You slowly become nutrient-deficient, even though you are eating regularly.

The second ominous trend is the *movement away from real, living food into dead, fake foods.* Ninety percent of what most of us eat on a daily basis is now fake food.

Years ago in their book *Fit for Life*, Harvey and Marilyn Diamond taught us that to live, we must eat living foods. Living foods like peaches, carrots, and apples have enzymes that keep us alive. Dead foods like potato chips, candy bars, and fettuccine alfredo have no enzymes and bring us closer to death.

Real food is fresh fruit, fresh vegetables, and raw nuts. And the meat eaters can argue with the vegetarians about eating flesh. But one thing we can say for certain: Dunkin' Donuts, Frosted Pop-Tarts, and M&M's are not real food. Cheetos, Fritos, and Doritos are not real food—even if it does say "made with real cheese" on the package (because, of course, cheese is not real food!). Hot fudge sundaes, stuffed-crust pan pizza, and rocky road ice cream are not real food. We have convinced ourselves (along with lots of help from advertising agencies) that things like cake and cookies and chips are real food. They're not.

The end result is we have become overfed, but malnourished.

Our bodies keep sending us messages saying, "I need more nutrients." So we feed it more. But we're feeding it so much dead and fake food, that we're still nutritionally deprived. Fake foods have little or no vitamins, minerals, enzymes, antioxidants, or fiber—all things that are vital to wellness. So our bodies ask for more and more. The end result: We are being "super-sized."

It started as an American trend. We made fast food an art form. But this American trend has morphed into a worldwide one.

I'm writing this chapter from aboard a Qantas 747 on the way from California to Australia. I took my first trip down under about eight years ago. Back then I marveled at how slim everyone in Australia seemed to be—just like I used to be able to sit and people-watch at the Café Ruc in Paris and be able to spot the Americans from a block away.

No longer. From Singapore to Moscow to Caracas, people have readily embraced the fast food/fake food diet, and their bellies, thighs, and extra chins are showing it. When the first McDonald's in Ljubljana, Slovenia, opened, people were lined up for miles to consume their first Big Mac.

I could recite the statistics on the increasing percentages of people who are overweight and clinically obese, but why bother? Numbers don't connect with people, and the percentages would be obsolete by the time this book gets into your hands. Here's all you really need to know, if you want to really understand what is happening:

Think about the size cookies were when you were growing up. If you're at least 30 years old, I bet they were about three inches across. Then they started creeping up to five inches. Now you can find them the size of a Frisbee.

When I started my illustrious career as a dishwasher at Mr. C's Pancake and Steak House on Midvale Boulevard in Madison, Wisconsin, soft drinks came in three sizes: 8 ounces, 12 ounces, and 14 ounces. Today, go through almost any drive-through and you will find the *small* is 14 or 16 ounces, the medium is 20, and the "best value" is 24 or even 32 ounces! One convenience store chain sells a 64-ounce soda. That is a bucket!

Growing up, my best friend was Ed Stack. Ed was a big boy and also the only person I knew in the entire world who could eat a whole Whopper from Burger King. In fact, when we went to Burger King, our other friends often came along just to witness someone eating the whole thing. Today the chain routinely runs promotions for double and triple Whoppers—value meals with extra large fries and sodas!

How much of your daily requirements of vitamins, minerals, enzymes, anti-oxidants, and fiber do you think you're getting when you consume a Frisbee-size cookie, a 64-ounce soda, or a triple Whopper? What percentage of your daily fat and cholesterol intake do you think you're getting?

Today it is quite common to see young children who already have serious weight issues. In fact, it's easy to find five- or six-year-olds who have never eaten a piece of real fruit. They went direct from baby food to Happy Meals. If you give them a bowl of ripe, delicious strawberries, their sense of taste is so out of whack that they need to cover the strawberries with refined sugar or whipped cream to make the berries palatable to them!

We are eating more and receiving fewer nutrients. We are getting bigger and bigger, but our actual standard of wellness is worse and worse. And as we age, we are paying a huge price for our lack of good nutrition in degenerative diseases, pain, and suffering. My grandfather, grandmother, and great aunt all lived to their mid-80s. But was the poor quality of life in their later years really worth it?

So what's the answer? How do we take back control of our bodies and claim the wellness that is our birthright? Well, we can start by planting our own gardens, growing our own organic produce, and singing "Kumbaya" together.

Right.

If you would swear off all fake food, and eat nothing but raw fruit, raw vegetables, and raw nuts, you'd be the peak specimen of physical health. The reality is, that isn't going to happen for most of us. The frenzied pace of today's lifestyle is not likely to lessen. In fact, you could argue that it will only speed up. Mothers used to spend eight hours roasting a turkey for the family's evening meal. Now they throw some processed turkey slices in the microwave for ninety seconds and impatiently wonder why "cooking dinner" is taking so long.

The real secret to wellness is some common sense and moderation. And realizing that if you watch five hours of television a night, you're going to easily view 25 or 40 commercials designed to keep you sick, fat, and lethargic. You must recognize and counterprogram against this subliminal brainwashing if you want to be healthy. And you'll have to really evaluate what you eat—what percentage is fake food, how much is addictive food, and what kind of preventive wellness activities you practice.

In the interest of disclosure, let me put this out front. I live in Miami, site of the original Krispy Kreme store on NE 6th Avenue. When I drive by, and that "Hot Donuts Now" sign starts flashing, I've been known to have problems with the steering on my car. When I change planes in Atlanta and I have to pass by the Cinnabon stand, I have sometimes succumbed to sins of the flesh. When I researched this chapter at Burger King, they were offering a new chocolate/banana shake—which I might or might not have tried.

Let's be realistic: When you're having a Super Bowl party at your place, your friends are probably not expecting you to serve alfalfa sprouts and tofu burgers. You no doubt have a busy lifestyle and will likely continue to consume meals on the go. But you can still be smart about it.

You need at least five servings a day of fresh fruit and vegetables. And no, peach cobbler, carrot cake, and strawberry Pop-Tarts don't count! Take the advice from the Diamonds' book and eat only fresh fruit before noon each day. This will load you up with precious enzymes and provide good fiber and lots of great nutrients. It also gives your digestive track a rest and provides you with greater elimination of toxins.

Always start with a fresh salad before your other meals. This will fill you up with some living food, and you'll eat less fake food. You'll eat less fat and keep your blood pressure and cholesterol at lower levels.

Stay away from refined white carbohydrates. Replace white breads with multigrain versions, and eat whole wheat pasta instead of enriched. Eat brown rice instead of white.

Eat four or five smaller meals instead of three large ones. Start each day with some exercise, even if it's just a walk around the block or 10 pushups. And most importantly, supplement your diet with vitamins, minerals, enzymes, fiber, and antioxidants. I can get away with my occasional pizza, cookie, or ice cream, because I take these kinds of supplements. And so can you.

You simply can't be happy and prosperous if you're not healthy. And once you truly experience optimum health, you'll be amazed at how much more energy you have for life, the great and creative ideas you come up with, and the resolve you have to go out and live life out loud, in vibrant color!

Make a commitment now to take back control of your body. And then let's explore how you handle your other challenges to stop being victimized and create your own abundant destiny . . .

CHAPTER 4

Letting Go
of Victimhood

■ ■ ■

**How You Fall into Victim Cycles—
and How You Break Out of Them**

■ ■ ■

What do all of the following statements have in common?

"Ever notice that as soon as you light up a cigarette, the bus comes?"

"I know I am forgiven, even though I don't deserve it, because Jesus died on the cross for my sins."

"When I was little, my father deserted us, and since then I have a hard time accepting love and affection."

"Just when I was getting caught up, my bitch ex-wife got my paycheck garnished for the unpaid child support."

"I was raped once, so now I am nervous around most men, and I can't get intimate with a man without it crossing my mind."

"I'd like to work, but as soon as someone sees my past conviction on the application, they're afraid to hire me."

"I'm all for personal growth and I'd like to attend that program. But my husband isn't into that stuff and he doesn't like me participating in it."

"I'd like to open a business of my own, but my wife doesn't like the idea. So I guess we'll just have to keep struggling, and I'll stay with my dead-end job."

What all of these statements have in common is the nature of the person making the statement. As diverse as all of those statements are and the people who make them would appear to be, each statement reflects the same type of person: a person with serious worthiness issues, low self-esteem, and a predisposition toward negative expectations.

But the biggest common denominator all these people share is that they are desperately holding on to *victimhood*. They almost celebrate the fact that they are being victimized. They entertain you with stories of the latest mishap, tragedy, or calamity that has befallen them. Of course, they're not really victims, but volunteers. They've made a choice—albeit usually a subconscious one—to remain a victim.

You can't be a victim and move forward in life. If your self-image is one of being victimized, and that's what you affirm to the people around you, you create a self-fulfilling prophesy. You will probably repel love, defer happiness, attract illness or injuries, and sabotage any financial or business success. You sell your victim story so well to everyone around you that you end up following the script exactly.

I was recently trading e-mails with an acquaintance on the subject of raising self-esteem and valuing yourself. As a child, this woman had been a victim of much horrific abuse. She mentioned this fact several times in our e-mail conversations, then got into the specifics. The advice I gave her was to never mention it to me ever again, or to anyone else, for that matter—except to a qualified therapist.

Once you have healed these kinds of issues with a mental health professional, you can talk about them in a way that can help others. You might appear on a television show, write a book about your experiences, or give keynote speeches on how to overcome these challenges. But in the meantime, talking to anyone about them other than a therapist is just an excuse to *hang on* to that victimhood. And that's an easy thing to do . . .

Why would so many people, all over the world, cling so desperately to situations that victimize them? Let me count the reasons:

1. They can tell themselves that any failures in their life are not their fault.
2. They can believe that outside factors are responsible for all bad things in their life, thus absolving them of personal responsibility.
3. They can get attention, sympathy, and pity from others.
4. They can substitute this attention, sympathy, and pity for the love they desperately need but don't know how to receive.
5. They can use past rejections to justify never getting emotionally close with anyone else.
6. They can use their past failures to justify never even attempting to achieve lofty goals or pursue noble projects.
7. They receive confirmation that they are a "sorry sinner," will "never amount to anything," or don't have the right education or connections to succeed.

8. They can feel heroic as the little guy or gal, fighting the forces of evil against all the odds.

9. They can feel spiritual, believing they are sacrificing happiness on the human plane, so they will receive their true reward in the afterlife.

10. They can just be basically unconscious, like most of the herd, and let life happen to them, without having to think.

What you've just read is the top 10 list of reasons people stay dumb, sick, and broke. No matter which of these reasons—or, more likely, combinations of these reasons—you believe, the end result is still the same: You will lead a one-dimensional life of meager subsistence, existing day to day, with no real shot at happiness and fulfillment. And that is a crime. And that's not the path you want to be on.

It would serve you well to study the list again (especially the last three). Then do some critical thinking to determine which ones you may have bought into, because identifying that you are holding on to victimhood is the first step to releasing it. Once victimhood is exposed, its emotional charge is negated.

However, to discover the cause, we must again look to early programming, and the core, foundational beliefs you developed in childhood. Those core beliefs shade the way you see everything that happens to you for your entire life. They determine what you expect, and thus what you actually manifest. There is an undeniable link between your programming, the core beliefs that programming creates, the vision you develop for yourself, and then the results you create in life.

This will likely put you on one of three possible cycles. The cycles are:

1. *The Midas touch*—everything you touch turns to gold, platinum, or Prada.
2. *The flat line*—every day is Groundhog Day, just getting by in your life of quiet desperation.
3. *The bottomless pit*—your life is in a constant downward spiral, each drama, trauma, and tragedy leading to the next.

Very few people move between these cycles. Most are stuck in one for most or all of their life. And very few are in the first one, the Midas touch. Most of the herd is trapped in the flat-line scenario, just trying to make it to the weekend so they can rent enough movies to zone out and forget about their tedious life until Monday morning— when they repeat the process all over again. And a smaller, but steadily growing group is trapped in the bottomless pit cycle, manifesting trauma and drama on an ongoing basis. They career from one misfortune and setback to the next, each time confirming their belief that life is a bitch and then you die.

They finally get that job interview they hoped for, then get a flat tire on the drive over and miss it. They win $4,000 in the lottery scratch-and-win game, but the money is seized for unpaid child support. Or they use the very last of their money to fix the transmission in their car, only to have the police impound it the next day because of unpaid parking tickets. They see all these unfortunate events as being created by outside circumstances.

You probably know someone like this. Or quite possibly *you* are someone like this.

Take a trip to any jail or prison and you will meet hundreds of people claiming to be victims of circumstance. Enter any big-city ghetto or barrio and you'll find the same thing. Likewise, if you stroll through a middle-class neighborhood in London or Lisbon, Cologne or Copenhagen, you will meet people who believe they are the result of their circumstances, good or bad.

They will talk about the opportunities they were given or the chances they were denied. They may be grateful for the education they were exposed to or bemoan the fact that they were denied one. One person will celebrate his upbringing while the other will decry hers.

Yes, income, status, caste, education, upbringing, neighborhood, family, and many other circumstances will influence, affect, and even determine your station in life. But *who creates the circumstances?*

Lost in all this analysis and the assumptions of the people just described is one very, very important reality: *the effect of thought on circumstance.*

In *As a Man Thinketh*, James Allen tells us that our minds are like a garden, which can be intelligently cultivated or allowed to run wild. In either event, the garden will *bring forth*. If you plant and tend your garden, it will produce flowers, fruits, vegetables—the things you purposely cultivate. If you don't plant specific seeds, then animals, wind, and other elements will cause random seeds to find their way into the soil, producing an abundance of weeds and wild vegetation, likely to choke out useful plants. One thing is certain: Something will grow in your garden.

Just as a gardener must tend his or her plot, keeping out the weeds, you must tend the garden of your mind, weeding out the thoughts of lack, limitation, and negativity. You must nurture and tend the thoughts of happiness, success, and purpose.

If you practice gardening of this kind, you will soon discover that you are the master gardener of your soul. You will come to the profound realization that you are not the victim of your circumstances, but the architect of them. For it is those thoughts you give precedence to that shape your character, create your circumstances, and determine your ultimate destiny.

The outer circumstances and environment of your life are directly connected to your inner state. The most important thing you can learn about success, prosperity, and happiness is that *thought and character are one.* No one simply wakes up one day in prison, or divorce court, or the emergency room. These events are the direct result of the thoughts you have had up to that point.

Now, if you are like most people, this is the part where you start to mentally make excuses for yourself. You believe that what I just said is true for other people most of the time, but you are quite certain that you have been the victim of extenuating circumstances beyond your control. I know—your situation is different. You're special.

Okay, you're allowed to think that—for a while. But let me tell you about me, because my situation was different. I was special.

I went through at least 11 negative, dysfunctional relationships with neurotic, jealous, and needy partners. In the first restaurant I owned, the guy my business partner and I hired to run it falsified the sales figures and kept 80 percent of the profits. In the hair salon I bought, my partner actually stole the fixtures one weekend and sold them. The tax authorities seized the pizzeria I owned. In each case, I was just the innocent victim, manipulated and injured by others, always fighting against the odds, blah, blah, blah . . .

Bullshit. I chose those relationships, I hired that manager, and I attracted my business partners, like I chose to start a business without enough capital and didn't pay my taxes.

You don't simply find yourself in jail, the hospital, or bankrupt, any more than you simply wake up happy, healthy, and rich. All these circumstances are reached as a result of thousands of little decisions, which are reached as a result of hundreds of thousands of thoughts.

I learned this the hard way. I was in California and had just had dinner with a couple whom I respected a great deal. I regaled them throughout the meal about the bad breaks, tough luck, and unfortunate circumstances that had been plaguing me. As we were getting into their car, Spence, the husband, said to me, "Have you given any thought to what you're doing to manifest all this?"

Well, I was simply devastated. How could this so-called friend be so insensitive, uncaring, and clueless? I couldn't believe he didn't understand and empathize with how I had been the innocent victim in all these unfortunate events.

I chewed on that for about three weeks before it finally dawned on me that Spence was right. It was an ugly realization—but also a liberating one, because once you get it, and you take ultimate responsibility for what is happening in your life, you suddenly understand that you have the power to change your course and create your dream life.

You must accept that, on one level or another, you have manifested everything happening in your life, even the horrific, nasty stuff. Of course, you don't do it consciously—but you do it.

It can seem like the injured party is an unfortunate victim of never-ending bad luck (especially when you are the injured party!). But, of course, all of these misfortunes are the result of bad choices made earlier. After all, the seemingly innocent victims are actually the ones who made the choices to avoid paying child support, ignore the parking tickets, defer maintenance on their car to buy cable TV, get into negative relationships, and make thousands of other poor decisions, which later come home to roost.

Of course, you make all these decisions based on your core beliefs. Then you enter a self-perpetuating cycle, making decisions that create results to support your expectations, thus validating your beliefs, which then play out all over again.

Letting Go of Victimhood

If you developed one of the common money beliefs in child-hood—some examples would be "Money is bad," "It's spiritual to be poor," or "Rich people are evil"—it will cloud your view of every financial transaction you are ever a part of. If someone offers you a partnership in their business, you might think they are likely to cheat you, so you pass it by. If you learn about a new business opportunity, you could never give it an honest evaluation, believing you need to know someone, get in at the top, or have a better education level to benefit from such an opportunity. If you have beliefs like "the rich get richer," you'll likely think investments are only for wealthy people and never make an investment yourself. So you'll always live paycheck to paycheck, at the mercy of outside forces.

I know, because I sabotaged myself with beliefs like these for 30 years. If ever there was anyone who could snatch defeat from the jaws of victory, I was that guy. I was always a day late, a dollar short; the one who got all the tough breaks, bad luck, and freak mishaps. I was the poster boy of the poor, downtrodden little guy always fighting the Man, the system, and the forces of evil.

Of course, what I came to discover is that I lived in a self-perpetuating cycle of victimhood. When bad things happened, I accepted them resignedly. When good things happened, I always looked for the cloud in the silver lining. And as a result, I always found it.

Unfortunately, I didn't have an exclusive on this. Today, millions of people around the world are still experiencing life in a similar way. They are unknowingly locked in this kind of victim pattern, subconsciously re-creating one bad experience after another, denying themselves the happiness, health, and prosperity they deserve. And it's quite likely you are one of them.

That doesn't mean you have to be homeless, on the street, an addict in a crack house, or subsisting on government assistance, although you could be. But it could mean you have to buy used cars instead of new, order from the right half of the menu, and decide which pizza place to call based on who is offering the best cents-off coupon.

It could mean that you can't scrape together the down payment to buy a home, or you refinanced your home to pay down your credit card debt, which you promptly ran up again. It may mean you don't have money set aside for your kid's college expenses, a retirement plan for yourself, or even a nest egg to protect you from an unexpected emergency.

You may have super-sized yourself into high cholesterol, diabetes, size XXL clothes, or even a heart attack or stroke. You could be repeating the same negative dysfunctional relationship over and over, with different partners but the same result.

You could be one of the millions of people maxed out on your credit cards, paying interest rates of 17, 19, or even 25 percent. And if you're paying the monthly minimum, you're signed up for the 40-year plan.

Or you might be in the other groups of victims: the people winning the rat race, but living like rats. People in this group have what most people think are good jobs or incomes, but the price they pay can't justify them. How many people lose their health because of a job? Pay someone else to raise their children? Destroy their marriage or other relationships to get ahead in business? Slave away at a job that gives them no satisfaction?

If you have a high salary but have to work 90 hours a week and ignore your loved ones to get that kind of money, that is not prosperity. Or if you carry a pager so that you're on call 24 hours a day, what kind of lifestyle is that? True prosperity means doing work that brings meaning and significance to your life. Grinding out a living is just subconsciously accepting victimhood.

Letting Go of Victimhood

Getting trapped in a cycle is the direct result of the programming you received early on. Three components work to create the cycle for you. Here is the process:

1. The programming you are exposed to creates your core, foundational beliefs.
2. These core beliefs help you develop your vision of your life.
3. Your vision creates results that conform to it.

As Allen tells us in *As a Man Thinketh*, your vision is the promise of what you shall one day be. So to break a negative cycle and create a positive one, you have to change your vision. But it's not that simple. Until you get back to the cause (your programming) and change the catalyst (your core beliefs), you won't be able to create a new, positive vision to move toward.

So how do you truly break out of a negative cycle? You have to start with all of the programming you're exposed to: the media influences we discussed, religious and government propaganda, and especially the people in your life.

Let's start with the media exposure you get. One of the best things you can do is to stop following the news. Don't watch it on TV, don't listen to it on the radio, and don't read about it in newspapers or magazines. News outlets make their money selling news. And bad news always sells better.

In an average newspaper, 90 percent or more of what you read is negative news. The percentage is about the same in the other media. And you don't need to know most of this news. Do you really believe it's important to find out how many houses burned down, people were killed, or cars were stolen last night? Being exposed to all of this negativity creates negative thought patterns in your mind.

When I tell people to skip the news, they invariably ask how they will know if and when the Japanese bomb Pearl Harbor again, a nasty hurricane is headed their way, or terrorists strike near them. Trust me, you will know about all of the big stuff you need to know about. Restaurants and shops now have TVs blaring the all-news networks, cab drivers want to tell you the latest bad news, and people at work inevitably talk about whatever the media is broadcasting. When something major happens, you won't be able to escape from it.

I haven't watched the news in at least 10 years. I get the newspaper to read the baseball section and Dilbert. The rest is just stuff designed to keep me dumb, sick, and broke, and I don't want to live there any more. Eliminate the news media from your life and you'll immediately eliminate a source of serious lack programming.

Then replace it with some positive programming. If you don't have them, get copies of *Think and Grow Rich*, by Napoleon Hill; *The Magic of Thinking Big*, by David Schwartz; and *As a Man Thinketh*, by James Allen. Buy some personal development CDs from Dr. Wayne Dyer, Deepak Chopra, and Lisa Jimenez. Then make a commitment to spend 30 minutes in daily self-development time. Do it in the morning, before you leave the house, so you create a positive consciousness throughout the day. Then take a couple of minutes for something positive just before you go to sleep at night.

It isn't enough just to stop some of the negative programming you're getting. You must counterprogram for all of the years of negative programming you've already received. You need to create new core beliefs, and you need positive programming to do that.

Become a critical thinker, and use those critical thinking skills when you're deciding what movies or TV shows to watch, what books to read, and which radio programs you'll listen to. Of the 60 or so network shows on television in a week, there are probably fewer than 5 you should consider watching. For every 10 blockbuster movies that come out, there might be one that isn't filled with negative subliminal programming.

That doesn't mean you have to move to a monastery, either. I have some guilty pleasures and you can, too. I think *The Sopranos* probably contains as much or more negative programming as any show on television. I mean we're talking about a show where the hero is a Mafia don. I also happen to think that it is the most brilliantly written and acted show that has ever been offered on television. So I watch it.

I'm sure I will go see *Spiderman III, IV,* and *V,* whenever they come out, because I've been a Spiderman fan since my childhood comic book days. But when I watch things like these, I am conscious of what the underlying programming is. And I make sure to give myself some extra positive programming, perhaps an extra 20 minutes reading something positive before bed that night. Make sure you do something similar.

If you belong to a religious group that teaches that you're not worthy and that it is spiritual to be poor, get out of it now. Find a spiritual community that celebrates who you are and teaches how to live in abundance—because that is the true order of the universe.

If you are struggling now, you have probably surrounded yourself with people who give you permission to stay where you are, or people who subconsciously want you to fail. You may even have people around you who *consciously* want you to fail. Get them out of your life, or reduce the amount of time you're exposed to them. Life is way too short—and too blessed—to live in any other way than prosperity.

I don't even like another common practice, people who are self-effacing or use self-deprecating humor. They use words, phrases, or jokes that make them appear less than they are. This is just like many victims do, but the motive is often to put others at ease or make a connection with people. Your subconscious mind still gets the negative programming in a situation like this.

My friend Richard Quick is the swimming coach for Stanford University and the U.S. Olympic team. He's probably helped put as many athletes on the medal podium as anyone alive. The first rule he tells his swimmers is no derogatory humor. He believes that if you hear something enough times, you start to believe it.

Give yourself more positive than negative programming every single day. Gradually you will start to change your core beliefs. (And don't beat yourself up because it doesn't happen in just a few weeks. You've had years to create the negative beliefs.) Once your core beliefs change for the better, you'll finally be able to craft the positive vision of the life you would love to live. And once you've done that, it's only a question of time before that vision manifests itself.

CHAPTER 5

The Metaphysical Element of Getting Rich

■ ■ ■

The Missing Link between Motivation and Manifestation

■ ■ ■

Metaphysics is the branch of philosophy that examines the nature of reality—in particular, the relationship between mind and matter. So let's explore how that relationship works in terms of prosperity consciousness—more specifically, how you go from being motivated about something to actually manifesting it in your life.

I've been dubbed "the Millionaire Messiah" because I believe you were born to be healthy, happy, and rich. People often ask if I really believe that everyone in the world can be wealthy. They believe wealth is limited, with not enough to go around for everybody. But true prosperity is limitless.

I really do believe everyone can have all the prosperity they desire. But the universal laws that govern prosperity can only do *for* you what they can do *through* you. So each of us will manifest our prosperity only to the degree that we understand the spiritual laws that govern that prosperity. And there are a lot of confused people in the world right now.

Emmet Fox stated, "The secret of successful living is to build up the mental equivalent that you want, and to get rid of, to expunge, the mental equivalent that you do not want."

So what does all this mean?

Prosperity is created in the mind first. All the good you wish to manifest already exists as an ideal in your mind on the superconscious level. Metaphysically speaking, this means that you already have the fulfillment of your prosperity—otherwise, you could not have desired it in the first place.

At this very second, in Infinite Mind, there are the ideas of abundance, vibrant health, your perfect vocation, and healthy relationships. Your villa in Rome, designer clothes, a red Lamborghini Diablo, or any other material manifestation of prosperity you desire is there as well. Your prosperity comes from the power stored within you, waiting for your demand.

Now, to manifest your good on the *physical* plane, it is necessary for you to build a bridge between these realms. You must open the channel for your good to appear. But before we go further, with all of this discussion of prosperity, you might find it helpful to know what I mean by the term.

True *prosperity* is loving relationships, fulfilling work, contributing to a greater good, beautiful sunsets, magnificent summer thunderstorms, abundant health, talking with good friends until two in the morning, rainbows, and the playful nature of a kitten. It is knowing where your good truly comes from and having a strong spiritual foundation in your life.

And . . . it is having an automobile that makes your heart race when you see it parked in the garage, beautiful homes in the places you love to be, a closet packed with enough shoes to give Imelda a run for her money, and enough bling-bling to make your heart sing-sing!

Now this may be quite different from what you've been taught in New Age prosperity circles. Some people will tell you that prosperity has nothing to do with money. That's just dumb.

Yes, I know money doesn't buy happiness. But it lubricates life and can prevent a whole lot of unhappiness. It is a lot easier to be happy if you're not worried about paying the rent, earning enough money to take care of your children, or having enough to eat. Having the money to pay for the braces on your kid's teeth, provide a home health aid for an elderly parent, or purchase your homeowner's insurance could sure prevent a lot of unhappiness. Poverty breeds unhappiness, hopelessness, and despair. It causes people to lie, cheat, steal, and even kill.

There are people going around teaching prosperity workshops who are broke. They say things like, "Well, I haven't manifested a lot in the material world, but I am very blessed with good health and wonderful relationships." They have to say that, because otherwise you might doubt their teachings when you see them climb into their 1973 Pinto hatchback.

Sorry, that dog don't hunt. Real prosperity means enjoying abundance in every sense of the word—which includes money, cars, homes, and other materialistic things as well as good health, a spiritual foundation, and strong relationships.

Now maybe you aren't into cars, but you like boats. Perhaps you're not an opera buff and would rather be at a Jimmy Buffett concert. Maybe flying first class isn't important to you, but being able to take your kids on dream vacations is. You get the idea: Prosperity means having the freedom to live life full-on, out loud, and in living color, doing the things that bring you joy. It means living without fear of paying bills, scrimping by, or depriving yourself of the things that bring happiness, fulfillment, and meaning to your life.

In my case that means a condo on the ocean in Florida, a flat in Paris, fast sports cars, season tickets for the opera, trips all over the world, working when I want, playing in four softball leagues, walk-in closets packed with designer clothes, work that challenges me, having wonderful people in my life *and* the time to spend with them, and a spiritual sanctuary that fulfills my needs.

Yes, I enjoy the rainbows, sunrises, spring showers, and all the free things in life. But the sunrises are better when you can watch them from your own balcony every morning, instead of once a year when you're on vacation. I've seen spectacular rainbows in Hawaii, Fiji, and Tahiti. How many poor people ever get that opportunity? It's pretty special when you can surprise someone for Valentine's Day with two first class tickets to Paris for dinner at the Four Seasons George V. Dare I say it might even make you a little happy?

Your true nature is not to be the person who struggles with credit card debt, dysfunctional relationships, or a dead-end job. You are a perfect individualization of Infinite Power. This Infinite Power created man in its image. I'm not particularly concerned what other label you may have for this Power. Whether you call it Universal Law, Allah, God, or Natural Order does not change what it is and does. You are the self-expression of the Infinite Power of the universe.

Read that last sentence again.

Because you are the manifestation of this Power—this Power is expressing itself as you—it cannot leave or forsake its own self-expression. Infinite Power is above you, below you, next to you, within you, and projecting itself as you.

That means that not only are you the image and likeness of this Power, but you are *forever one with this Power*. You and this Power can never be separated. And once you understand this at every level of your consciousness, your true awakening has arrived. Your prosperity is already completed in the mind of Infinite Power. As a co-creator in this realm, you simply must manifest prosperity in the physical realm.

This Infinite Power expresses itself as you, me, and everyone (and everything) else on the planet (and millions of other planets). So how, then, can we define this expression?

As consciousness.

Consciousness expresses itself as consciousness. Put another way, Infinite Mind expresses itself as mind, Infinite Love expresses itself as love, and Infinite Prosperity expresses itself as prosperity in you.

So when you manifest prosperity, you are doing no more than demonstrating the expression of your spiritual consciousness—your true nature—which is the expression of Infinite Power as you.

So what does that mean in practical application? It means that God, nature, the universe, or whatever you prefer to call this Power does not give you a new car, a better job, or a bigger home. Nor does this Power withhold your good, give you disease, or limit your prosperity. Infinite Power simply gives each of us itself. It gives us substance—and substance becomes the new car, better job, or bigger home. To manifest prosperity—whether that is optimum health, great wealth, or attracting your perfect soul mate—you must tune in to the prosperity consciousness that is inherent in your true self.

This Power within you is responsive to your needs. Once you learn how to tap into this Power, you can manifest all the prosperity that is yours, because you actually are this Power in expression.

This Power is in all people. But it does not reveal itself until the host person develops his/her consciousness enough to access it. The supply ever awaits your demand on it. The demand must be made before the supply can come forth to fill it.

Tapping into your success and prosperity has almost nothing to do with opportunity, chance, or luck—or even training, education, or skill. It's all about developing your consciousness to become one with your true nature. When I was sick, broke, and unhappy, I was a high school dropout, with no formal education, connections, or training. Now that I am healthy, rich, and happy, I'm still a high school dropout, with no formal education, connections, or training. The difference between then and now is my consciousness.

This is not New Age mumbo-jumbo. Although accessing true prosperity must be done within a spiritual context, the spiritual laws that govern prosperity are actually very scientific and quite tangible. They are based on value-for-value exchange and provide the highest good for all concerned. The only free cheese is in the mousetrap.

The world has many examples of enlightened people who have walked the earth as human, yet demonstrated this spiritual Power. Buddha, Gandhi, Sathya Sai Baba, Jesus Christ, and many others have demonstrated that we are meant to be healthy, happy, and prosperous. If you are struggling with challenges right now, it may sound crazy to hear that you were born to be rich. But that is your true nature. In fact, being poor really is a sin.

For you Biblical scholars, if you go back to the original definition of *sin* in the Aramaic language, it means "to miss the mark." Or if you have ever studied *A Course in Miracles*, you know that the Course defines *sin* as "a lack of love." I'm okay with either of those definitions, because I believe that if you are not manifesting abundance, you are missing both the mark and the love that this Infinite Power has for you—or, in more metaphysical terms, the love *you* have for you!

Many people suffer in lack because they hold on to an erroneous belief in the Power that runs the universe. They subscribe to the cosmic Santa Claus theory, believing in a God who is making a list and checking it twice, gonna find out who's naughty and nice. Do you really think that God is up there somewhere, sitting behind big pearly gates, dictating, "Well, Joey is a good guy, give him a Lamborghini. David is okay; let him have a new Toyota. But Becky is having an affair—she'll have to settle for a beat-up Ford Escort."

We are all co-creators with God/Power/Universe, because God/Power/Universe is us. When we miss the mark, it is not because there is a vindictive Power withholding what we want from us. It is because we turned away from our own divinity, our own power. The reason Becky is driving a beat-up Escort is not because a vindictive God is punishing her for having an affair. She is punishing herself by doing something that causes her guilt and lowers her self-esteem and expectations for herself, creating worthiness issues and starting a negative cycle.

Prosperity is not being withheld from her. She has simply turned away from it, not believing herself deserving of it. Like millions of others, she doesn't know that she has the power to produce her own prosperity by living in accord with certain spiritual laws. (I explore these in Chapter 7.) There is so much lack in the world today because there is so much self-hate. Clear up your understanding of your true nature and your prosperity will appear.

In his landmark book, *Prosperity*, Charles Fillmore reveals an important insight right in the Introduction. He tells us that we have a wise and competent Creator, who provided for all our needs. Two key points:

1. Our Creator provided for us with a spiritual substance, which is around us everywhere.
2. This substance responds to the mind of man. It is your thoughts that manifest the substance into day-to-day reality.

Substance doesn't come from "up there." You don't have to search for it and you don't have to get more of it. It is all right here, waiting for you to summon it.

You never have an idea you can't manifest—if you did, the universe would be weak at its most critical point. When you transform this substance into earthbound prosperity, it's not because God/Power/Universe heard your request and granted it. Your faith is the key that unleashes the power within you that transcends human limitation.

So how do we convert this substance in the ethers into our prosperity? Through ideas.

Everything has its origins in the mind. Ideas are the center of consciousness. Infinite Mind is a repository of ideas for the resource of man. Your health, relationships, intelligence, and finances are determined by the ideas you give your attention to. What you become is a result of the efforts you expend to collect these ideas.

One nurse works in a hospital and reaches the highest pay allowed in the compensation scale. She bemoans her lack of opportunity and settles for mediocrity. Another nurse in the same situation has the idea to apply her skills to open her own home health care agency. She goes on to abundance, because she used an idea to mold substance to her good. Both nurses have this power, but only one developed the consciousness to accept it.

Consciousness creates your mind-set, which is what we will explore next.

CHAPTER 6

Creating Your Prosperity Mind-Set

■ ■ ■

How to Think like the Ultra Rich

■ ■ ■

I was sitting in the back of a pedicab, traveling down Duval Street in Key West. We turned right onto Fleming Street, and I was hoping my driver would pedal a little faster, as the rain looked imminent.

Suddenly he stopped. A rooster and four baby chicks crossed the street just in front of us. A dad taking his kids for a Sunday stroll. Only in Margaritaville!

My driver was a student from Ecuador, spending his summer visiting friends and earning a few bucks pedaling lazy tourists like me around. We got within a few blocks of my guesthouse when the downpour began. He pedaled furiously and finally got us under a large tree in front of my place. I gave him $20 and dashed inside. But not before seeing his eyes light up like a Christmas tree.

Of course, everything is relative. If I was on my way somewhere and in a hurry, I might not stoop over to pick up a twenty on the sidewalk. To this exchange student working his way through summer vacation, that $20 bill was probably the highlight of his day. And the rel-ativity continues up the ladder. I can feel prosperous about buying a pair of shoes for five grand. But Richard Branson spends about that much every month to keep fresh flowers in his homes.

As I flew back from Zurich recently, Delta Airlines offered the movie *Wall Street* on the classic movie channel. There was a scene where Charlie Sheen looks at a painting and comments that Gordon Gekko (Michael Douglas) must have been taken when he bought it. Daryl Hannah points out that the painting cost $400,000.

"Four hundred thousand dollars!" he exclaims. "You could buy a whole beach house for that!"

"Maybe in New Jersey," she sniffs.

How you view these stories and situations like them says a great deal about your outlook on life—and the prosperity consciousness you approach life with.

I recently went to see a movie with a friend. As we waited in the concession line, he commented that since a bottle of water was $2.50—the same price as a small Coke—he was going to order the water. His thinking was that the cost to the theater was higher for the bottled water than the fountain soda. Now, he wanted a Coke, but he ordered a bottle of water, because he felt that the water would cost the theater more. This was his way of getting back at the theater for charging exorbitant prices.

Does that strike you as prosperity consciousness or lack-based thinking?

I have another friend with a retail business. For a long time, the first thing you would see when you went to the counter was the paint peeling on the back wall. For two years I ragged on him to sand it down and paint over it. He steadfastly refused, because the peeling paint was the result of some previous seepage from the outside of the wall, and he wanted his landlady to pay for it. She had refused, saying that the inside wall was his responsibility. Finally, after three years of back and forth, including my friend's threatening to fix the wall and deduct the cost from his rent check, she relented and had it repaired. Cost: less than $150.

So after three years, my friend feels vindicated, because his wall is painted, and he didn't have to pay for it. Meanwhile, how many hours did he spend on this drama? And what kind of impression was he making on all of his customers for those three years?

Everything we have discussed so far has to do with mind-set. A person's mind-set dictates whether he's comfortable spending $5,000 a month for fresh flowers, while others would hesitate to spend that much on a car. It explains why some people earn $25,000 a year, while others pay 10 times that much just for their annual country club dues.

Mind-set is a fascinating thing, because it doesn't just come into play for the things you buy. Your mind-set will also dramatically affect how you view your earning and profit potential, and the wellness or disease you manifest. Mind-set determines what you believe you can accomplish, and what you expect from your relationships. What your money mind-set is will be pretty consistent with the way you view other forms of prosperity.

When I am talking to potential team members for my business, I mention that they have a chance at unlimited income potential. But no one actually gets the concept of *unlimited*. If they have been making $20,000 a year, they equate unlimited income with earning $30,000 or $40,000 a year. If they are used to taking home $65,000, they think unlimited is making $100,000. And if they are used to being paid $100,000 annually, then they probably envision about $200,000 as unlimited income. The degree to which they see "unlimited" in money matters is directly related to how they will also view their prospects in health, relationships, success, and happiness.

What this escalating ladder of expectations demonstrates is how people's consciousness can expand. And that is what has to happen with you for you to develop a prosperous mindset. It is a continuous process that never stops.

You start out thinking that $75 is an outrageous amount to pay for a floral arrangement. Gradually you begin to see the beauty of a $150 arrangement. Next you are thinking it would be nice to have some fresh flowers delivered to your home each week. Next thing you know, you're spending $1,500 a month on fresh flowers—and loving it, because you appreciate the beauty it brings into your world.

When I was conducting a Mastermind retreat in Las Vegas, one of the shops in our hotel had a purse that cost $10,000. Now, I'm not personally into purses, but I know this: Every woman in my group talked about that purse the whole week. I have to believe it would bring great joy to the owner.

Could you spend $10,000 on a purse, a pair of shoes, or a beautiful coat? Can you see yourself spending $15,000 for a first class seat, instead of $700 in coach? Do you believe you could spend $450,000 for a painting to hang in your living room or a sculpture to place in your entranceway? Of course, everything is relative. If you make $20,000 a year, it would be crazy to spend 10 grand on a purse. But then again, why would you make $20,000 a year when you could earn so much more?

Creating true prosperity consciousness is about expanding your vision of what can be for you. Abundant people see opportunity. They never think something is too good to be true. They expect good things.

People with prosperity consciousness are dreamers. They imagine a better way, then work to make it so. More importantly, they don't buy into the negative and erroneous beliefs around them. When they are told something is too difficult or not possible, they simply smile at the thought. They are not easily swayed by the cowardly cautions of the herd.

It's not that those in the herd are lying. They honestly believe that things can't be done. They don't know the difference between facts and beliefs.

Let's say a single guy moves to Detroit. He goes to a nightclub and asks a girl to dance. She looks him up and down and says, "With you? I don't think so." He beats a speedy retreat back home to nurse his wounds. A few days later he tries another nightclub and a different girl. He gets rejected again. This is all the "proof" he needs to illustrate the "fact" that ladies in Detroit are stuck-up.

Another guy moves to Detroit the same week. In his building's elevator, he meets the couple who live in the apartment next door, and they invite him over for dinner. A few days later, his car breaks down and a passing motorist stops to offer him assistance. He becomes convinced of the "fact" that people in Detroit are friendly and welcoming.

So which guy knows the truth?

Well, in each case, it is the truth as they know it. But in neither case is the truth they know actually fact. Both guys have developed a belief. One has a belief that serves him; the other has one that does not. Each will probably attract more of what he expects, and each will likely fall prey to confirmation bias, finding continuing "evidence" to support his belief.

How you will react to any situations that come up is determined almost entirely by your mind-set. Take my friend Matt. We stopped at a fried chicken joint to eat after our ballgame one night. As we were walking up to the door, he said, "You know what's going to happen? I bet they are going to be out of chicken! That happened to me once. I went in and they were out of chicken. How can a chicken place be out of chicken?"

So what happened? We went in. I ordered a three-piece chicken dinner, which I got. He ordered a three-piece spicy chicken dinner— which, of course they were out of. He looked at me and raised his arms, as if to say, "I told you so."

Now we could do a whole lesson on how he manifested them being out of chicken. But that's for another day. The point I'm raising here is his mind-set. He expects bad things to happen to him, so they usually do. I love him, but he must affirm 300 bad statements every day. I am constantly stopping him in mid-sentence, screaming, "Wait, you are about to affirm something bad!" And he pauses for a second, thinks about it, and finally says something like, "Well it's true though. My suitcase always *is* the last one off the plane."

Fascinating, isn't it? Your mind-set colors how you view every situation you encounter every day. And it shapes the way you attract things into your life.

Some people are predisposed to think they will be wildly successful, some figure they will get by, and others like Matt expect the worst to happen. Your expectations will color how you view each situation you encounter, hundreds of times a day. That in turn will color how you act in each situation. And each one of those small, seemingly insignificant decisions determines your future.

If you think the rich get richer, and you have to have money to make money, you will probably do nothing to break out of being broke. You will think you want to be wealthy, but on a subconscious level, you will just tell yourself it would be a wasted effort.

If you think that good things only happen to other people, you won't expect them to happen to you. And when they do, you won't even recognize them, because you're not expecting them. You won't accept when people want to do good things for you. That may manifest as something simple, like refusing their offer to help you with a project, or something much larger, like refusing to accept unconditional love from someone who cares about you. You could pass up a great investment opportunity, decline to open a business that can make you wealthy, not protect your health, or even repel your perfect soul mate. Or all of the above.

Of course the opposite is true, too. If you believe you are worthy of wealth and happiness, you will expect good things to happen. And when they do, you will accept them gratefully. When you get presented with lucrative opportunities, you are likely to act on them. And when you have a chance to try something really bold, daring, and monumental—you will go for it!

There are seven keys to creating a mind-set for prosperity. Let's look at them.

Key 1: Recognize and Release Victim and Entitlement Mentality

We talked about this a great deal in Chapter 4. Some more thoughts on the topic: You are going to continually be tempted to backslide into the victim mentality, because it gets you such good support and acceptance from most people. They will invite you to commiserate as to how you have been victimized, so they can then share their victim experience with you. This creates a negative feedback loop that keeps you justifying failure instead of seeking success.

Beware also of the entitlement trap. This could come in the form of college aid, special government grants, or a wealthy relative advising you that you're in their Will. Once you know that you could be eligible to receive something, it's a short step to thinking you're entitled to it. And entitlement has nothing to do with prosperity. True prosperity is always a value-for-value exchange.

Key 2: Recognize and Reject Jealousy and Envy Mentality

This one is another easy trap to fall into, particularly when you're exposed to the media. Their job is to build people up and then tear them down. It makes for great entertainment and keeps the public engrossed. You have to stay away from this, as it demeans good people and fosters self-hate, doubt, and jealousy.

Take the Martha Stewart situation: Did she actually conduct insider trading? I don't know; I wasn't there. But I know the relentless media coverage of her trial, incarceration, and release was dripping with pettiness, jealousy, and lack. The fact that a housewife could go on to build a billion-dollar company was simply too much for reporters and media personalities to handle. So they either portrayed her as a monstrous danger to the public safety, or treated her as a target for mean-spirited ridicule.

A similar thing happened with Jack Welch from General Electric, one of the most successful CEOs of our time. He also wrote a book, which became an international bestseller. So when his financial details became public in divorce filings, the press had a field day. His economic success fit perfectly with the "CEOs are over-paid" meme.

If you read the crap the media dishes up on Stewart, Welch, and other successful people, you can become influenced by the slant of the reporting and secretly take some delight in these icons being brought down to size. But this is just hateful gossip masquerading as news, and it is anti prosperity. Being jealous of someone else's success is fear-based and blocks your own prosperity. Celebrating others' success comes from love, and this attracts more prosperity to you.

Key 3: Understand the Infinite Nature of Prosperity

If you are like most people, you think paying $10,000 for a coat or $15,000 for a plane ticket is obscene and, in fact, deprives others from their good. You'd quite likely feel like the money is being kept from a nobler purpose, such as giving it to your church, saving the rainforest, or sending it to a relief agency to help poor people in Africa.

Here is the problem with that belief: It is based on the assumption that money is finite. But like all forms of prosperity, money is infinite. Love is infinite. Hugs are infinite. Joy is infinite. Wellness is infinite. And so is wealth.

So it is not a case of having to choose one or the other. You can buy a $10,000 coat *and* be the top contributor in your church. You can spring for the first class ticket *and* send money to the starving children. Once you develop the right prosperity consciousness, your abundance—and your ability to do good with it—grows every year.

Key 4: Build Your Sacred Circle of People Who Nurture and Support Your Highest Good

One of the most important things you can ever do for success is to consciously select your mentors and partners. Remember what Jim Rohn said about the five people you spend the most time with. I call this your *sacred circle*, because the people in this inner circle of yours are going to dramatically impact all areas of your life.

If you're married or living with someone, one of your five spots is already taken. If you work all day closely beside someone, another slot is filled. So if those two slots aren't bringing you up, you better look very carefully at who fills the remaining ones!

You may also want to have some extended mentors. In my case, I am mentored by Bill Gates, Richard Branson, Larry Ellison, Warren Buffett, Napoleon Hill, J. Paul Getty, Andrew Carnegie, and others. They just don't know it. But I study everything about or by these people that I can find. They have achieved a level of success I'm striving for, so I want to know how they think. Look for people who are where you want to be and learn all you can about them.

Key 5: Seek Out Abundance Environments and Limit Your Time in Lack Surroundings

One reason a lot of people live lives of quiet desperation is because they feel that the sacrifices necessary for success are not worth it. They mistakenly believe that to become successful they'll have to give up drinking, smoking, swearing, drugs, TV, nightclubs, and so on, and lead lives fit for a monastery. The reality is a sensible balance can take you far.

Going to a nightclub or having a few drinks occasionally is not likely to keep you from being successful. However, hanging out in bars or nightclubs on a regular basis could certainly curtail your growth and advancement—because of the people you're likely to be surrounded by.

Savvy prosperity students place themselves in abundance environments where they are surrounded with people of higher consciousness. You could spend Friday evening at a pulsating disco or the Barnes and Noble café. Where do you think you'd find more success-oriented people?

Look for churches like Science of Mind and Unity that offer a variety of classes and workshops, and you are likely to meet many positive people. Likewise for business, success, and health seminars that come to your area. People who attend these are people dedicated to growth, and that's a good environment to place yourself in.

Key 6: Practice a Daily Self-Development Program

As we discussed earlier, daily self-development time is critical to expand and maintain a strong prosperity consciousness. Even if the TV shows and movies you watch, the people you hang out with, and the books you read are mostly positive, you are still going to be assaulted with tons of negative and limiting programming. It's vital that you counter-program with something positive every day. Don't go out of the house until you have a bulletproof mind-set for success and happiness.

Don't leave this to chance or whim. Structure and schedule self-development time for first thing every morning. Make sure you include things like this book that foster critical thinking skills.

Your subconscious mind can be programmed and is most receptive when you are in an alpha state. An alpha mind state is that relaxed, dreamy feeling, where you aren't quite sure if you are awake or asleep. You go through several alpha states during the course of a night's sleep, so you may want to play CDs that project subliminal positive affirmations while you're sleeping. You can find the ones I use in the Resources section in the back of the book.

You can also access an alpha state during meditation or massage. During this time you can play subliminal CDs, create your own recording of affirmations, or just use the time for positive visualization. Train your subconscious to work for you and you will have a powerful ally.

Key 7: Know Not Just What You Are Moving Away From But Also What You Are Moving Toward

Okay, you know you don't want to be poor any longer. Or you decide to get out of a negative relationship. It may not be enough to simply want to be rid of a bad situation, for you may find yourself simply repeating negative patterns. It's important that you create a new vision of what you want to move towards.

I'm a big believer in creating Prosperity Maps of the things you want to do, have, and become. (You'll find more information about them at the special web site we've created for readers of this book in the Resources section at the back.) Also helpful are goal cards, notes on the mirror, and other items that remind you what you are moving toward. Affirmations are a great resource to remind you what is important.

All seven of these key actions help to program the good you want to create into your subconscious mind. Once your subconscious mind has a goal to shoot for, it won't stop working until that goal is achieved. Next, we'll look at the spiritual laws you must be in accord with to make your prosperity a reality . . .

CHAPTER 7

The Universal Laws that Govern Prosperity

∎ ∎ ∎

Laws You Must Live By to Manifest True Abundance

∎ ∎ ∎

There is an interesting undercurrent running through this book so far, one that you've probably had your own thoughts about: the issue of God, universal law, nature, or Innate Power. More specifically, the issue of whether such a force exists, and if so, what is it?

This topic reminds me of a fascinating dinner I once attended. It started out with a large group, but eventually wound down to just a few: a fundamentalist Christian, a Jew, an agnostic, an atheist, a new-thought Christian, and me. So naturally I couldn't resist bringing up the delicious issue of religion and whether God exists.

It should come as no surprise to you that, even though we talked till way past the restaurant's closing time, we didn't definitively settle the issue. But what a captivating and enthralling conversation ensued! Exactly the kind of discourse I relish.

Here was the fascinating thing to me. I do believe in a power greater than myself. But as the discussion bounced back and forth—primarily between the fundamentalist Christian and the agnostic and atheist—I kept nodding in agreement with most everything the two nonbelievers had to say.

Why? Because they had come to their beliefs after a great deal of introspection, critical analysis, and conscious thought. In contrast, my fundamentalist friend just kept parroting the inane clichés she had learned at eight years old in her Catholic school, claiming these clichés were "proof" of God, because the Bible said so.

Of course, from a rational, logical point of view, the idea of God existing is impossible to substantiate.

Now, notice that I said from a rational and logical basis. That does not mean that God does not exist (although a strong argument can be made that he/she does not). What it does mean is that the proof of God existing cannot be determined using rational thinking or logical reasoning.

Now, fundamentalists, before you write to me, please make sure you really understand the meaning of those two words, *rational and logical*. Just because Psalm 14:1 says, "The fool says in his heart, 'There is no God,'" does not qualify as being consistent with reason and intellect. Nor do the other 25 scripture verses you want to quote me to supposedly prove that God exists.

I could write quite a book here refuting the different ways theists try to prove that God exists. In general, their beliefs can be categorized into three schools of thought.

First would be natural theology: We can't explain everything in the universe and how it got here, therefore there must be a supernatural being or force behind it all.

Second would be the cosmological arguments: Every existing thing has a cause, and every existing cause must be caused by a prior cause. So either we have an endless chain of prior causes, or we had one first cause, namely, "In the beginning, God created the heavens and the earth."

Third would be the design arguments. These are centered around the premise that everything in nature occurs by design, so we must conclude that there was a master designer, something or someone omnipotent and omniscient (God).

As I said, I could write a book refuting all three of these arguments on a rational, logical basis, demonstrating they cannot be proven. I could, but I have neither the time nor inclination to prove or disprove the existence of God. The point I'm making is that the usual "evidence" theists trot out to prove the existence of God in reality proves nothing.

The reason I kept nodding in agreement with many of the things my agnostic and atheist friends were saying that evening is because they made such a convincing case for their beliefs, and it was obvious they had come by their beliefs after a great deal of critical thought. It should be noted that the atheist is a former minister who graduated from Oral Roberts University. He came to his beliefs after many years of soul searching, research, and study.

So while I don't agree with his conclusions, he has my utmost respect, because he is not just parroting something organized religion programmed into him when he was six years old. He's a brilliant guy who came to his decision after conscious introspection. In fact, you will find that quite a large number of intellectual heavyweights are agnostic or atheist.

I came to the issue from the other end of the spectrum. I was an atheist for the first 26 or 27 years of my life. After some serious introspection, and what I believe was a spiritual revelation (and my atheist friends would probably view as mystical hallucination), I came to believe in a Higher Power.

My problem with my fundamentalist Christian friend (which is the same problem I have with fundamentalists of all faiths) is not just the arrogance and intolerance of her beliefs, but the fact that she is just repeating the script programmed into her by the nuns in the Catholic school she attended. She didn't come to her beliefs through conscious thought or personal choice, and she is afraid to question them. Had she been born and raised in Iran, Pakistan, or some other country, she would likely be covering her face in public, wearing a burka, and preaching how the infidel Christians are actually Satan in disguise.

I do believe in a God. I don't harbor the delusion that his or her existence can be proven with rational evidence—at least not at our current level of scientific understanding on this human plane of existence. But the important thing is this: I could be wrong!

Maybe there is a God, maybe there is no God. It *doesn't matter* in the context of what we are discussing here. It could be that what I call "God" is actually nature, universal order, or some other system of evolution. What matters is that there is *something* that causes specific reactions to actions you and I take. And these reactions are predictable.

I believe what we're discussing here are universal laws. But whatever they are, they work and hold true. When you operate in accord with these laws, you will receive predictable results. I can tell you that the discovery and implementation of these laws allowed me to turn my life around from abject poverty to abundant riches. I share them here in the hope you will give them a test-drive and discover the results for yourself.

So, having said that, here are the seven universal laws I believe you must be in accord with to manifest prosperity in your world.

Law 1: The Vacuum Law

If you walk down the beach, you leave footprints in the sand. But give the wind and the waves a few minutes and those tracks will be filled in, just as vegetation will cover a field, and an agenda expands to the time budgeted for a meeting.

Nature abhors a vacuum. And since the inherent nature of the universe is good, a vacuum will always be filled with good. So one of the fastest ways to manifest prosperity in your life is to create vacuums.

One evening at the end of the prosperity class I was teaching, one of the students walked up to me, confused. She wanted to know how all "this prosperity stuff" could be working, since she had recently lost both her job and her boyfriend.

The interesting thing was that she had been complaining about that job for months. Her pay had been minuscule, and the job had offered no room for advancement. And several times we had discussed her boyfriend, who had been both physically and verbally abusive to her.

I pointed out to her that getting rid of two negatives in her life meant she was quite likely on a very positive path toward prosperity—which is exactly how it turned out for her. As her consciousness developed, her job could no longer hold her, and her boyfriend was no longer comfortable with her. Ultimately, she was able to get a much better job and attract a man who appreciated her—without the abuse.

If you hold on to the negative, there is no room for the positive to come into your life. So when people come to me for advice because they are not manifesting true prosperity in their lives, the first question I ask them is this: What are you holding on to that you need to release?

This principle applies to attracting prosperity in all areas of your life. If you want some new shoes, give away some of the ones you have. If you want some new clothes, clean out your closet and donate those clothes to the homeless shelter. Create a vacuum. Want some more hugs in your life? Want more love in your life? Give some away!

Of course, this same law applies to health. I had a lot of health challenges the first 30 years of my life, just like I had a lot of financial challenges and other personal issues. The bottom line is that I was dumb, sick, and broke, and I couldn't understand why.

I came to discover that, in actuality, I was manifesting all that lack in my life because I had a victim consciousness. I was holding on to lack, because it allowed me to keep manifesting bad things . . . which allowed me to feed my noble victim scenario.

I could hang around with all my loser friends each day, and we could all commiserate about how hard it was to get ahead, how rich people had all the opportunities, how unfair life was, and other such nonsense.

I was *holding on to being a victim*—so there was no space in my mind for me to become a victor. Once I was able to let go of my victimhood, a whole new world of possibilities opened up for me. Health challenges I had carried around my whole life just cleared up at the snap of my fingers.

Don't get me wrong. The health problems were real, and I had all kinds of medical records, sick days, and doctor visits to prove it. But they were real because I believed they were real—and because I needed them in order to hold on to being a victim. Once I no longer desired to be a victim, my body was able to do what it was designed to.

It takes a certain amount of faith to practice this law. You have to be willing to let go of what you have now. Once you realize the universe is inherently good, it's easier to have faith in just outcomes. You no longer fear releasing a bad work situation, a negative relationship or a harmful belief, because you know they will be replaced with something of equal or even greater value.

You are surrounded by good everywhere. The only lack is the lack in your mind. Open your mind to receive prosperity, create a vacuum to give it room, and you will attract prosperity to fill that space.

Law 2: The Circulation Law

Think of prosperity as a brisk, flowing river. The water never stands still, but is always moving forward, releasing pressure, seeking its proper level. Now picture an eddy on that river, where the water pools in one place, stationary and stagnant.

The law of circulation that governs prosperity operates the same way. Miserly hoarding leads to recession. When you circulate substance, you break the energy block and keep the river of prosperity flowing freely.

For example, I never feel that I own anything, even though the title may be in my name. Even my cars and home are just in my life for a while. Eventually I will release them and move on. We all go through cycles. The house that you need when you are single may not be adequate when your three children arrive. Likewise when they grow up and leave home, you may wish for another, cozier abode.

You safeguard and use possessions when you have them. When they no longer serve you, you release them to someone else to serve. So I may sell one of my sports cars when I want to buy the new model. That serves both the new owners and me. I get my new car, and they get a car that is new to them, but at a lower price than a new model would cost.

It seems every six months or a year, I upgrade to a new computer, because the newer models have more and better features, are lighter, and work faster. So I buy a new one and give my old computer to a friend who doesn't have one. When you are practicing the first law and want to create a vacuum by giving away old shoes or clothes, you are invoking the second law as well.

Circulation of money brings powerful prosperity results. Let's suppose that you are in a bad financial situation. You are down to your last $100, and you have $1,500 in debts. Instead of hanging on to the $100, waiting for $1,400 to appear, you put the circulation law into practice. You know that miserly hoarding leads to recession. So you break the energy block by circulating what substance you have.

You tithe $10 to the source of your spiritual nourishment. Then you send a partial payment of $20 to the phone company, $15 to the electric company, $25 to one of your credit card companies, and so on. This breaks up the stagnant energy and gets your money circulating. Because you are circulating money, you create an energy that attracts more substance back to you.

When you are hanging on to that $100, you are creating a mindset (and energy) of lack, because you are focusing on that "last" $100. When you circulate it, you send your mind and the universe a message that more is on the way, and you then attract it.

Need I tell you that you can do the same thing with love? Send love forth in circulation, and you will attract much more of it back into your life. Give away something you are no longer using and get ready to receive your good.

Law 3: The Imaging Law

Prosperity, like all forms of success, is created in the mind first. When you image things in your conscious mind, you are actually

106

programming your subconscious mind to manifest them on the physical plane.

I'm a big believer in affirmations, goal cards, positive statements in your day planner, writing a movie script of your perfect day, or even sticky notes with affirmations on your steering wheel, mirror, or refrigerator. When you see these reminders, you think about the thing you are trying to manifest, and that emotion anchors the thought in your subconscious mind.

The more emotions you engage, the clearer the picture of what you want becomes in your mind. And the clearer that picture is to you, the sooner you will manifest the real thing. (Remember what you learned back in Chapter 1 about how emotions help the effectiveness of memes.)

THE PROSPERITY MANIFESTATION MAP . . .

Earlier I mentioned the Prosperity Manifestation Map. These are a lot of fun and very powerful tools for creating your prosperity. Here is a little more information on how to use one.

Fill your Manifestation Map with photos, graphics, and affirmations of things you want to manifest in your life. I like to divide mine into sections, such as work, spiritual, relationships, and so on. Then in each area, put images on the map to represent things you want to do, have, or become. So, for a couple of weeks before you do this, start collecting magazines, brochures, and other materials about whatever interests you.

Suppose you want to learn to play the guitar. You put a photo of a guitar, perhaps one from a music magazine, on your map. But not just any guitar. You put the exact model you want to play on.

Let's say your goal is to be closer to God. You might put a religious symbol, a religious affirmation, or a particular scripture or quote on the map.

Maybe you want to write a best-selling book. You might cut out the *New York Times* bestseller list and white out the number one book and type in the title of yours. Or you could type your name on a list of your company's biggest producers, or Academy Award winners, or *Forbes* magazine's richest people on the planet, and so on.

There are no rules for how you put things on the map, except that the image has to mean something to you. It doesn't matter if anyone else understands it. They don't need to. But you have to know what it means every time you see it.

Back when I was still struggling, I saw a commercial for the Dodge Viper. I was almost shell-shocked with how beautiful the car was, and I knew I had to own one. About a year later, I learned about Prosperity Manifestation Maps and did my first one. I just knew I wanted a red Viper. However, the only picture I could find was of a black one, so even though I wanted a red Viper, I used the picture I had.

A few months later, while negotiating a consulting contract, I put a clause into the contract that when their sales reached $2 million a month, they had to buy me a new Viper. And then an interesting scenario unfolded . . .

Even before the company's sales reached the level stipulated in the contract, the president of the company called me. He was so happy with the rapid progress we were making, he wanted to buy me the Viper early. He had a friend who was the largest Viper dealer in the world, and he could get a special deal.

It seems a casino owner in Las Vegas was going through a divorce, and he had to raise some cash fast. He had a Viper with the special accessory package, exotic rims, and some body modifications made by the company that designed the Viper prototype for Dodge. This Viper was the only one of its kind in the world.

There was just one problem: It was black. So my client wanted to know if I would be happy with this special, one-of-a-kind Viper, or did I still want a red one? I felt conflicted and asked for some time to think.

I went out for a bike ride down Ocean Drive. About halfway down, I came across two Vipers parked at the valet stand in front of a restaurant—one red, one black. Coincidence, right? I got off my bike and walked around them. I looked and looked at them from every angle. And I decided I had to have a black one.

Since then I've had four Vipers, and the original black one is still my favorite. As I look back on the whole experience, I am sure that the reason I had to have black is because I put that black photo on my Prosperity Manifestation Map.

In just a two-year period, I manifested everything that was on my Map—and I had some pretty bold, audacious goals on there. So I can't encourage you strongly enough to create your own. Place it where other people won't see it (so negative people can't ridicule it) but where you will see it every day. Just walking by and catching sight of your map with your peripheral vision will have a powerful and positive effect on you.

Seeing the images every day literally programs them into your subconscious mind. This creates a desire within you to take the daily actions that bring your dreams closer to reality. Image your prosperity in your mind first. Then manifest it on the physical plane!

Law 4: The Law of Ideas

In Chapter 5, you learned that we manifest prosperity from the ethers by the power of ideas. If you can think of an idea, you can manifest it. Otherwise the universe would be weak at its most critical point.

There is abundance at every spot on earth. It doesn't come from "up there." You don't have to search for it and you don't have to "get" more of it. It is all right here, waiting for you to summon it.

When you transform this substance into earthbound prosperity, it's not because God/Power/Universe heard your request and granted it. You imaged it, believed you were worthy of it, and then put your subconscious mind in charge of figuring out how to make that happen. This is how you create ideas. And ideas are what manifest prosperity on this plane.

Everything has its origins in the mind. Ideas are the center of consciousness. Your health, relationships, intelligence, and finances are determined by the ideas you give your attention to. What you become is a result of the efforts you expend to collect these ideas. When I wrote the Viper clause into my consulting contract, that came from an idea I had for manifesting my good. You are limited in what you can manifest only by the ideas you come up with. It all depends on how you think.

On my *Prosperity* audio album, I refer to this law as "The Creativity Law." That's because it's all about using your creativity to pay bills, manifest wealth, and create desirable outcomes. Sometimes it's as simple as changing the way you think about something.

About 15 years ago, my business was struggling. We had fallen behind with some of our creditors. Every week my vice president would come into my office with a big accordion file labeled "Bills" and we would decide whom and what to pay.

After weeks of this, I finally had a revelation. Each "bill" we had was really an invoice for a blessing we had already received. For instance, when you get a bill from the power company, it's because they kept you warm in the winter or cool in the summer, and gave you light to live by.

We threw away that file, got a new one, and wrote "Blessings" on it. Then we started writing an affirmation on the envelope of every invoice that came in: "I give thanks for your immediate and complete payment." It changed the whole energy of the process.

We had fallen into a siege mentality. Every day when the mail came, we dreaded it and had started to see the creditors as our enemy. The new folder and affirmations turned everything around. We realized again that our creditors were our partners. We talked to everyone, worked out payment plans, they worked with us, and in a few months, we were completely up to date with everyone.

The universe is substance, and this substance is available at all times to those who have learned to lay hold of its consciousness. Once you are aware of this—and you know that you have been provided with the mind to attract it—manifestation of prosperity is simply a case of developing the right ideas.

Law 5: The Law of Reciprocity

As you've probably noticed, these seven laws are interrelated. The Law of Reciprocity stands above them all as "the law of laws," because it is the fundamental operating principle of the universe.

Everything in prosperity is a value-for-value equation. But the wonderful part of that equation is that what you give comes back to you multiplied. You can never outgive the universe. The more you give, the more you get back.

You've also heard this law described as reaping what you sow. When you receive your blessings, it's important that you celebrate and share them. If you have a gift (whether that is playing the piano, teaching, or painting) and you don't practice it, you are shortchanging your true nature. To honor your innate abilities, you must celebrate and share them. And as you do this, you attract even more blessings into your life.

All true actions are governed by this law. Nothing just happens. There is really no such thing as luck or chance. All happenings are the result of some cause and can be explained in the law of reciprocity. We doubt this when we don't know the cause of something, but it is always there. What we see as miracles are things controlled by causes we don't yet understand.

Now, just as you can attract and multiply your good, unfortunately, it can work the other way as well. Let's suppose that you gossip about a co-worker. You are creating a negative karma debt that must be paid. And that return also comes back in multiples.

Every circumstance in your life right now is the result of causes you created. So if you want to change your circumstances, change what you are giving out. Give only good and you will get back only good.

If you doubt me, try this experiment: Go out and smile at everyone you meet tomorrow. Tell someone her hair looks nice. Pay the toll for the car behind you. Go out of your way to hold the elevator or open the door for someone. Send a check (even a small one) to a charity. Bring a token gift to some clerical worker who assists you. Call at least five people you love and tell them so. Offer to help an elderly person with his groceries. I guarantee you that you will receive blessings back in multiples.

Law 6: The Law of Tithing

Imagine if I made you this offer: I will have American Express issue a second card for my account with your name on it. You can use this card anywhere it is accepted, and you can buy anything you like. There is no spending limit. If you want to buy a new wardrobe, you can. If you pick out matching Ferraris and throw in a Bentley, that's cool. You can even buy a new house if you can find a developer who accepts credit cards. You can buy absolutely anything you want!

This is the only condition: When the bill comes every month, you have to pay 10 percent of it. So buy whatever you want; just know that you pay 10 cents on the dollar.

Now is that a great deal or what? Wouldn't you jump at an opportunity like that? Well, you already have one! It's called the *Universe Express* card.

Tithing is a spiritual law dating back thousands of years. It is simply the action of giving back to the source of your spiritual sustenance, usually your church, temple, mosque, or synagogue. The word *tithe* comes from Latin and means "tenth." Tithing is giving back 10 percent of whatever comes to you.

This is different from randomly sowing seeds, and also different from the money you give to charity. The principle behind tithing is that you give it back to the spiritual source where you receive your sustenance.

Tithing is one of the laws that most people seem to have difficulty accepting, especially agnostics and atheists. Most see it as a plot by the church to raise funds. And I'll be the first to admit that tithing certainly takes a leap of faith. It's not my job here to sell you on whether there is a God or not. That's not my calling and none of my business. I am just sharing what I know about living by the universal laws to manifest prosperity. And tithing is one of them.

Besides the atheists and agnostics, those people who believe in God but don't have a regular place of worship also question if and where they should tithe. You're a big kid, so I will leave it up to you, other than to say that your 10 percent should go to the source of your spiritual nourishment.

If you're hesitant about tithing, perhaps it will help if I share my story. I never tithed for the first 30 years of my life. I thought I was saving money. Hardly. I used to make $11,000, $15,000, or $20,000 a year. Now I tithe many times more than that.

I began tithing only after my life started breaking down and I started reevaluating everything. My business had been seized by the tax authorities for nonpayment of taxes. That put me $55,000 in debt, and I had no job, no car, and no bank account. I had been borrowing money to live on from friends for weeks, and those sources were drying up.

I was down to my last $20 when someone recommended that I buy the book, *The Dynamic Laws of Prosperity*, by Catherine Ponder. I think it was $12. If I bought it, I would be down to eight bucks. So the choice I faced was to either buy 80 boxes of macaroni and be able to eat for another 23 days, or get the book and have enough food for only eight.

I decided that if I was going to die of starvation, it was better to get it over with quickly. So I took a chance on the book . . .

In it, Reverend Ponder said I had to tithe if I wanted to manifest prosperity in my life. I was so desperate to believe her, I did. So out of my last eight bucks, I put one in the basket at church. (And I forlornly watched it go all the way down the aisle.)

The next day I received a check from the electric company for $75. The letter with it explained that they had been reviewing their records and because I was such a good customer who paid on time, they no longer needed a deposit from me.

Now, that was amazing, because I had to be one of the worst deadbeat customers they'd ever had. I paid my bill late every month, and they had actually turned off my lights for nonpayment three times. I was (and am) convinced that I got that refund because I tithed at church that Sunday. However, if you think about it, since I got the check on Monday, it must have been mailed the previous Friday, two days before I gave that dollar in church.

So how do I explain it? *I can't.*

All I know is I was afraid not to tithe after that check came, so I tithed on that check. And a guy who had owed me $200 for two years and had disappeared, suddenly reappeared and paid me. So I tithed on that.

I've been tithing 10 percent of every dollar I have ever made since then. And every single year I earn more than the year before. Only now I don't tithe out of fear. I tithe joyfully, lovingly, and gratefully.

When I talk about tithing, one question always comes up: "Is that 10 percent of the net or the gross?" The gross. Yes, the amount you received before paying taxes.

You never know how your tithe will come back to you. Money is a pretty common way. But it could also come in the form of reconciliation with someone you're estranged from, a gift, a new relationship, a healing, or a promotion. There are many ways your good can come back to you.

Here's what I also believe: The universe will always get its tithe. You can tithe voluntarily or by force, but you will always pay. All those years I never tithed, I was always having my car break down, losing paychecks, incurring medical bills, and going through every other conceivable drama and trauma to keep me broke. In a metaphysical sense, I now believe that I was having to pay extra things, which then circulated that money to people who were living by the universal laws.

Prosperity is about circulation. You have to keep your substance circulating or it gets stagnant. When you tithe by choice, you invoke many of the other laws, creating ripples of reciprocity that eventually find their way back to you.

Law 7: The Law of Forgiveness

You read my story of getting shot by the crack addict. Now learn the ending . . .

I woke up in the recovery room, with the doctor hovering over my bed. He told me they had had a hard time finding the bullet in my body, but had finally removed it. Then he casually mentioned that as long as they were in there, they took out my appendix.

"What! Why would you do that?" I asked. "The gunshot wound was on the other side."

"Oh, it's just standard procedure," he replied. "Whenever we open anyone up for anything, we take the appendix out as a precaution. That way you won't have problems later. You don't need it anyway."

I was incredulous. I simply couldn't imagine the arrogance and audacity of someone who thought they knew better than my creator as to which organs I needed in my body and would cut something out without even asking me.

I left the hospital a few days later with a great deal of resentment. To make matters worse, the surgery didn't work out very well. One day I looked down to see blood all over my shirt. The sutures had come undone, which necessitated another trip to the hospital. A week after that, the wound became infected, requiring another hospital visit. And the pain was unbearable. It didn't matter whether I was lying down, sitting, or standing. I couldn't find a position that relieved the agony.

As the months wore on, I seemed to be worse, not better. I woke up four or five times a night in a cold sweat. I had no energy, and my body seemed to be always fighting off an infection. I took trip after trip to my doctor. We tested for everything, but not one test came back positive. He admitted to being completely stumped as to the cause of my problems, so he started sending me to specialists.

We thought perhaps I had caught some tropical disease on my travels, so I went to an infectious disease specialist. No luck. We tried an ear, nose, and throat guy. Nothing. I saw a whole gang of other specialists. Nothing there.

Somewhere during all this I began to feel an intuition about what the problem might be.

"Doctor, I'd like you to X-ray me," I said one day. "I think the surgeon must have left the bullet inside me. I feel like my body is trying to expel a foreign matter."

"Save your money," he replied. "They're crazy at Jackson Memorial Hospital, but not that crazy."

Finally I went to a gastroenterologist, who wanted me to do an entire upper and lower GI series. As I was getting ready, the nurse noticed my scar and inquired about the cause. After I told her about the surgery for the gunshot wound, she went ahead with my testing.

About 20 minutes later, she came back in, holding up my X-ray. "I see they left the bullet inside you," she said, as though this was normal. "Is that because it's located right next to your spine?"

Imagine my shock, then anger. I had been sick for months and months. I had no insurance and had spent a small fortune on doctor visits, tests, and medicine. I couldn't remember the last time I'd had a good night's sleep. And to think the doctor had actually told me they took the bullet out. Why would he do that?

I was very confused and not sure where to turn. I had malpractice lawyers lined up 10 deep to take my case. It looked like a sure-fire out-of-court settlement for a million dollars easy.

But this happened after I had discovered *The Dynamic Laws of Prosperity*. So, like I always did when I needed guidance, I just closed my eyes, flipped open the pages of the book, and stuck my finger in to select a passage to read.

It was on forgiveness.

Ponder actually discussed specific situations, such as bringing a lawsuit against someone. She said that if you were holding on to resentment or revenge, you couldn't be open to receiving all your allotment of prosperity. I saw my million dollars swirling down the drain.

But intuitively, I knew what she said had to be true. I spent about 30 minutes meditating on the situation. I realized that the doctors and medical team had taken out my appendix and left the bullet in for whatever reason. But they had also saved my life. I had been taken to the hospital after losing a great deal of blood, my pulse was dropping, and my heart had almost stopped beating. If they hadn't intervened, I would have died within hours. I realized that they had done the best they could with what they had to work with and the consciousness they were at.

I wrote out an affirmation of forgiveness 13 times and put it in my Bible to pray on. I released the resentment and viewed the doctors and medical people in the light of God. And an amazing thing happened. That night, I got a complete night's sleep, straight through without waking up, for the first time since I'd been shot. I soon had another operation to have the bullet removed. But my health started improving dramatically the very day I forgave.

This law is closely tied to the vacuum law. If you are holding on to revenge, love can't walk in. If you are hanging on to resentment, you are hanging on to being a victim. And if you are holding on to being a victim, there's no space in your mind to be a victor. You must release the negative feelings, as they only eat you up inside and prevent you from manifesting your good.

Who do you think most people have the hardest time forgiving? If you answered "themselves," you get an A+. When someone comes to me and their prosperity seems blocked, this is where I look first. Once they forgive themselves, prosperity opens up to them.

So there are three steps I recommend you take right now:

1. Mentally forgive everyone you are out of harmony with.
2. Mentally ask for forgiveness from the people you have wronged in the past, have gossiped about, or are involved in lawsuits or other disharmony with.
3. If you have accused yourself of failure or mistakes—forgive yourself.

If you cannot forgive, you cannot accept abundance. However if you apply these three steps, you open yourself up for your highest good.

These seven laws are guidelines for living an abundant life. When you are in accord with them, you are in accord with the universe and will live a life of harmony, joy, and prosperity. Next, we'll look at some specific ways you can apply them to create wealth . . .

CHAPTER 8

The Greatest Prosperity Secret

▪ ▪ ▪

Unleashing the Awesome Power of Leverage

▪ ▪ ▪

O nce you have the proper mind-set, and you live your life in accord with the laws that govern prosperity, I believe you will achieve prosperity in whatever you do. Having said that, I also believe that you can achieve wealth easier and a lot quicker, if you engage in certain business models.

Notice I say *business models,* not *jobs.* While some people can create wealth working for others, it is does not happen often. Being your own boss usually gives you a much better track for becoming rich. The other common thread running through the three business models I recommend is that they employ the concept of leverage— and leverage is probably the greatest secret for amassing great wealth.

If you study the wealthiest individuals in history, people like Carnegie, Getty, and Gates, you'll always find some form of leverage in their success. Leverage is important, because without it, you're simply trading hours for money. Even if you have what many people would consider a good job, you may be just trading hours to get paid. And the problem is there usually aren't enough hours to get rich.

If you are a dentist, nurse, or doctor, your income is going to be directly tied to how many patients you can see in a day. Likewise, if you are an accountant, attorney, or consultant, you're limited by the number of clients you can work with.

This is the situation with most jobs, and a great deal of businesses. If you work five days, you get paid for that. If you stay home one day, you get paid only for four. Many businesses place a death grip on your life.

When I was in the restaurant business, I usually worked about 80 to 90 hours a week and often went weeks at a time without taking a day off. Anyone who has ever owned a restaurant, nightclub, beauty salon, retail store, or many similar businesses will understand exactly what I mean. You don't own the business—the business owns you.

The other problem with many traditional businesses is their dependence on you for the day-to-day operations, thus making them very difficult to resell. When a potential buyer sees how critical your presence is to the ongoing success of the business, they want to pay a lot less money for it—or may back out of a deal entirely. These kinds of situations are all missing leverage.

Leverage lets you escape the trading-hours-for-money trap. Leverage can be applied to your skills, knowledge, and expertise. And leverage can also be applied to your money. The more areas in which you can apply leverage, the faster you will be able to create wealth.

So let's look at the three best business models for applying leverage.

Business Model 1: Real Estate

I like this model because it lets you dramatically leverage your money. You can buy $100,000 worth of house for only $10,000 worth of cash. Once you have a portfolio built, real estate puts your money to work. You can leverage your money to buy more property, and then once you have it, you can use that property to let your money work more. And it can work two ways: First is the appreciation you can earn as your property increases in value. Second is the ongoing income you can earn from renting out your properties.

You have a few options when you're working with real estate. One is buying depressed properties, fixing them up, and then selling them for a quick profit—known as the "fix and flip." Option two is buying properties, fixing them up, and then renting them out. When this is done right, you have cash flow from the property, and you are also building equity in it, thereby increasing your wealth. A third option is actual development. You might buy vacant land and build housing, office space, or retail properties (or a combination) on it.

There are some qualifications if you want to follow this business model. First, you can leverage your money, but you do need a moderate amount of money to start. I realize many people out there are promoting "how to buy real estate with no money down," and this can be done, but I don't think doing so is prudent. You can't borrow your way to prosperity.

And while it can make sense to leverage your money, overleveraging is dangerous, because you have no room for error. Some unexpected maintenance, a natural disaster, or a prolonged period without a tenant could cause you to lose your property and move backwards on your track to wealth.

The next qualification is knowledge. Please don't jump into this business model without some training and guidance from a knowledgeable source. When you are buying properties to flip or rent out, having knowledge of the location in which you want to buy—its history as well as the current and projected market—is vital. If you buy in the wrong neighborhood as an investment, you could find property values actually going down. You have to understand how cash flow works and know that your property offers an opportunity for a positive flow. As for being a property developer, this involves serious money and knowledge and is not for the novice.

So, for this business model, I think it's a good one if you already have some cash flow coming in that you need to invest and put it to work—and you have some of the training and guidance required to do it in a profitable way. If not, then pass this one by for now.

Business Model 2: Information Entrepreneur

Would you like to be a wealthy Internet tycoon, working from home, writing from sidewalk cafés in Paris, or e-mailing your promotions by laptop from under a palm tree in Hawaii? (Imagine the thrill of checking your inbox each morning to find dozens of orders that came in while you were sleeping.)

Would you like to be a published author, signing your books for eager readers, and have a library of other resources like CDs, DVDs, booklets, Special Reports, and digital products? (Imagine the pride you'll feel the first time you see your book in a bookstore or your CD album on a client's bookshelf.)

Have you ever dreamed of being a professional speaker, giving workshops around the world to adoring crowds? (Imagine basking in a standing ovation, then watching the stampede of people rushing to your display table to buy your books, CDs, and videos.)

Well, if you answered yes to any or all of these questions, then you'll love a career as an information entrepreneur. This is a very exciting field. It's still quite young and absolutely exploding, thanks to the Internet, which offers a bold new way to operate and reach prospects. Basically, what you are doing is selling your information, expertise, or skills.

This business model is perfect for:

- People fed up with the rat race, who want to start a home-based Internet business.
- Writers who have finally realized that giving away all their information in $20 books is keeping them broke.
- Professional speakers who are stuck in the broken business model of chasing after a different audience for speeches every week.
- Computer geeks who want to know how to actually make serious money with their skills.
- Consultants who are caught in the trading-hours-for-money trap.

Of course, you could be someone who isn't in any of these fields, but who just has information in a particular area you want to market. That's fine too. The most important thing is that you have experience and knowledge that others are willing to pay for.

However, I really must warn you: The key words there are *others are willing to pay for*. When it comes to making money, academic knowledge is almost meaningless. The fact that you are the world's preeminent expert on caribou migration, solar eclipses, or the mating habits of aardvarks doesn't get it.

If you want to make money, your information must be tangible, practical, real-world stuff that people can implement to advance their career, improve their sex life, enhance their relationships, expand their skills, train their pet, raise their kids better, or something else useful. And, of course, the business world will pay big money for information on raising sales, handling mergers, managing employees, upgrading customer service, developing leadership, and so on.

Some examples of areas already demonstrated to offer lucrative potential for information entrepreneurs are:

- Marketing
- Sexual enhancement
- Home-based business
- Music
- Recruiting
- Sports
- Leadership
- Real estate investing
- Health and wellness
- Antiques
- Internet marketing
- Weight loss
- Sales
- Crafts
- Art
- Network Marketing
- Pets
- Investing
- Fashion
- Wealth building
- Spiritual enlightenment
- Finding good employees
- Marketing strategies
- Aircraft and flying

- Relationships
- Collectibles of all kinds
- Web site design
- Gardening
- Raising a family
- Interior design
- Nutrition
- Travel
- Presentation skills

And thousands of other skills, hobbies, and areas of interest!

Your topic does not have to appeal to a mass market, either. In fact, often the most lucrative situations are found in tightly targeting niche markets. Because these niches are under the radar, the cost of reaching prospects is minimal, and competition is almost nonexistent.

One Internet marketer built a solid cash flow by seeking out small niche markets like people who want to teach their parrots how to talk. A friend of mine did likewise with an e-book for people who want to know how to make toasts at weddings, dinners, and other social events. The key is to have an introductory product to get prospects into the pipeline, then keep providing new products as you continue to build your customer base.

WHY BEING AN INFORMATION ENTREPRENEUR IS SUCH A COOL, ENJOYABLE, AND PROFITABLE BUSINESS

The business is fun. It lets you take knowledge you have learned and experiences you have gone through and sell them to other people for money—for *a lot* of money. Speakers can easily get $5,000 or $7,500 a speech. The great ones make $20,000 and up. A one- or two-day seminar can earn you anywhere from $25,000 to $150,000.

And information products have a very fat margin, because people are not paying for the production cost but for the value of the content. A Special Report can cost you $1 to produce, yet sell for $47. A CD album may cost you $10 in production costs, but sell all day long for $147. Digital products (like e-books) are created for pennies, yet can sell for hundreds of dollars. The value is not in what these products cost to produce; it's in what people can do with the information contained in them.

As an information entrepreneur, you choose your own hours and where you work. Your only real concern is having a place with a good Internet connection. So you can spend the spring in Paris, the summer in Europe, and the winter in Hawaii or Fiji, if that's what you like. Follow your heart and the sun, living a lifestyle most people would kill for.

Now that's all the delicious stuff. But, like real estate, there are some qualifications here. First is the one we already discussed: You need to have the knowledge, skills, or experience someone would pay you to learn. But most people do have something others will pay for. If you do, this business allows you to leverage that.

With this business model, as well, you do need a modest amount of money to begin, but probably not nearly as much as you might think. I built a multimillion-dollar information marketing business with very little capital. And you can often presell your products before you finish producing them. Still, you definitely need some money to market what you have to your target audience.

You will also need to develop certain skills and acquire some critical knowledge. That knowledge will be in two areas. First, the production side of things: You'll need to learn how to secure a studio and record a CD or DVD, develop an e-book, and get resources duplicated, and you'll need to understand the many aspects of product development. You don't want to get into the business without learning all the critical information in this area.

The other area in which you must develop strong skills for this business model is marketing. To be really successful in this business, you must know about copy writing, direct mail, web site design, packaging, pricing, and other important marketing skill sets. So, like real estate, this business is not for novices. But if you have some money to invest and are willing to learn these skills, then the rewards can be extraordinary. And you can practice leverage to create serious wealth.

Now if you think this is a business model you'd like to follow, do your homework and get the training you need. I've put some links on the book web site for this as well.

Business Model 3: Multi-Level or Network Marketing

I love real estate and I want to build a huge portfolio. I've made ridiculous amounts of profit with it in very short periods of time. And I love being an information entrepreneur as well. I've earned millions doing it, and the lifestyle it provides is perfect for me. But my very favorite business, and the one I recommend to everyone, is our third business model.

Multi-Level or Network Marketing (also sometimes called MLM) is the last bastion left in the free enterprise system where the average person—without a large investment, vast experience, or a lot of education—can still create wealth. Many people with no college education, big war chests, or powerful connections have built fortunes in Network Marketing (myself included).

Imagine living in your dream house, driving your dream cars, and living your dream lifestyle. Spending quality time with the people who add quality to your life. Doing work with meaning, building your wealth as you help others reach their dreams as well. This doesn't have to be a dream. It has become a reality for many people who have built a home-based network marketing business.

In about 10 or 12 hours a week, you can build a lucrative business from your spare bedroom or kitchen table. You choose the hours you work and the people you work with, which makes it perfect for people juggling family schedules and other personal obligations.

You get great tax advantages and you also have the opportunity to travel to fun and exciting destinations. The income potential is unlimited and, even better, you earn residual income, the best kind of all.

You'll love building your business because you'll be helping others build success also. You have the rewards and independence of being your own boss, yet still enjoy the training, resources, and support of a major corporate support structure behind you. It's like owning a franchise, but without paying the large franchise start-up investment and ongoing royalty fees. And while a majority of the population is faced with money challenges, your business is poised for long-term growth opportunities.

By the way, I am *not* talking about pyramids, chain letters, or Ponzi schemes. Those kinds of get-rich-quick scams have been around for thousands of years and will probably be around for thousands more. What I'm discussing here is the powerful and proven network marketing business model.

The business actually began in the late 1950s with the pioneer companies of Shaklee and Amway. Others like Nu Skin, Herbalife, AVON, Melaleuca, Agel, and Mary Kay continued the evolution. For the last 20 years, the industry has steadily developed, actually growing 91 percent in the past decade.

The Greatest Prosperity Secret

Today, the network marketing/direct selling industry spans the globe, is practiced in more than 100 countries, and is still growing. Fifty-three million people participate and will produce estimated revenues this year of $100 billion worldwide—$30 billion of that in the U.S. alone. Is it any wonder that investors like Warren Buffett and companies like Virgin, Remington Industries, Sara Lee, and Time Warner are buying direct selling/network marketing companies?

In fact, Buffett's Berkshire Hathaway holding company now owns *three* direct sales companies. And Buffett said, "Dollar for dollar, it's the best investment I've ever made." *Fortune* magazine called the industry "the best kept secret in the business world."

Buffett and *Fortune* are not alone. Robert Kiyosaki, author of the *Rich Dad, Poor Dad* series, is another champion of the industry. He states that the business "gives people the opportunity with very low risk and very low financial commitment to build their own income-generating asset and acquire great wealth."

Another author touting the benefits of the industry is David Bach. David is the author of the best-selling book, *The Automatic Millionaire*. In his new book, *Start Late, Finish Rich*, he gives 13 reasons to join the industry:

1. The moment you join a direct selling company you're in business.
2. You don't have to reinvent the wheel.
3. You don't have to do it all by yourself.
4. You will be forced to stretch yourself.
5. You will find mentors and experts.
6. You can create passive income.
7. You may make a new circle of friends.
8. You don't have to retire.

9. You get to help other people.
10. You make your own hours.
11. Tax incentives!
12. Is less expensive to get in than many other businesses.
13. It's a family business.

Famed economist Paul Zane Pilzer also speaks up for the industry in his latest book, *The Next Millionaires*. He forecasts that 10 million new millionaires will be created in the United States over the next decade and predicts that many of them will be created through Network Marketing.

Like the other two business models, you need some training. But in Network Marketing, you have a whole sponsorship line of people above you who have a vested interest in the growth of your business. They are happy to train you for free. And the investment is ridiculously tiny, while the upside is extraordinary.

One of the surefire ways to create great wealth is to put yourself in front of powerful, emerging trends. Both Network Marketing and the work-at-home option are experiencing dramatic growth right now. It doesn't matter whether you have four university degrees or are a high school dropout. You can build a residual income money machine with Network Marketing.

I promote this business model over the other two for a couple of important reasons. First, it offers a much lower level of entry cost. For $1,000 or $1,500, you can acquire a full-fledged business that can produce serious cash flow. Second, the learning curve is much faster to traverse, and you have people who actually want and are rewarded for training you (whereas in the other business models, you basically have a bunch of competitors who want to eat you for lunch).

Leverage Your Leverage . . .

Now let me tell you what you could do to seriously turbo-charge your wealth and prosperity. Start a network marketing business and create a strong residual income cash machine. Then invest some of that money each month in financing an information entrepreneur business, and use part of that income to purchase some real estate. You use the first business to create cash flow, and the other two to get that cash flow working for you. You actually leverage your leverage. You are putting the greatest prosperity secret to work, and doing so exponentially!

Now that we have discussed ways of creating wealth, we must talk about how to protect it from the forces determined to wrestle it away from you. We must explore the virtues of selfishness . . .

CHAPTER 9

The Merits of Selfishness

■ ■ ■

The Need for Enlightened Self-Interest

■ ■ ■

The room is filled with the smooth, sensual sound of your favorite music. Burning candles give off a soothing glow, and the sweet aroma of your chosen incense gently scents the air. You step into the glorious, steamy water and sink down into your new hot tub. You settle for a moment, allowing your body to become accustomed to the heat, and then you reach over and turn a switch. Bubbles surge around you as the thrust and hum of the jets come to life.

The jetting water massages all your aching joints, teasing the tension of the day into a distant memory. You sigh—a deep, prolonged release of pleasure as every nerve relaxes into sweet oblivion. You smile to yourself and close your eyes, letting the steam and heat envelop you. The phone is turned off, so you won't be disturbed by anyone. The evening is yours—the perfect end to a brilliantly rewarding day.

Isn't it deliciously wonderful to be selfish?

Actually, if you're like most people, the mere thought of doing something selfish leaves you consumed with guilt. However, selfishness is your moral prerogative.

Isn't that why the phone's turned off—so no one can bother you? No call from your mother complaining about her condo association members, no plea from your friend Nick asking you to help him move, or Julia wanting a ride out to the airport, or the guys asking to watch the game on your new flat-screen HDTV.

If it feels so good to be selfish, why does the very word make us flush with guilt? Ayn Rand wrote a book titled *The Virtue of Selfishness*. When asked why she chose to use a word that threatened so many people, she replied, "For the reason that makes you afraid of it."

Like Rand, I also use the word *selfishness* to describe virtuous qualities of character. The dictionary definition is basically "concern with one's own interests, without regard for others." That means you value yourself first, regardless of what anyone else thinks. Notice that there is no good or evil implicit in the definition. "Without regard for others" does not mean that you are doing harm to others. It simply means that you are well-adjusted and sensible enough to meet your own needs first.

Of course that's not what most of society, or the herd, would have you believe. They tell you that your moral imperative is to put the interests of the many before the interests of the one, that you should sacrifice yourself for the greater good.

This idea is very dangerous to your self-esteem and your life. Relinquishing your happiness for the sake of others, whether they are known or unknown to you, verifies to yourself, and others, that you are small and unworthy of even your own attention. Subjugating your happiness to others is actually anti humanity, and it makes you mentally sick.

The Merits of Selfishness

Your survival and your pursuit of happiness must form the foundation of your value system—to design your life, by your own means, with your own standards, and for your own enjoyment. Anything less than that is harmful to you. And anything harmful to the individual is actually detrimental to society as a whole.

But don't think society is smart enough to figure that out. It isn't. The herd will maintain that the needs of the individual should be relinquished to the needs of the many. They tell you it is your responsibility to take care of the less fortunate. Sounds innocent enough, doesn't it? Well, let's take a look . . .

One Saturday you're out watering your lawn when a car drives up and you recognize your old friend Eddie at the wheel. You learn that he has just lost his job, his wife has kicked him out, and he couldn't think of anywhere else to go.

Eddie always seems to be in the middle of some drama or another, which is the main reason you haven't spoken to him for a while. But you feel sorry for him and invite him to crash for the night. The next day, Eddie asks if you wouldn't mind if he stays just a couple more nights until he can find an apartment, and he assures you that he has a job all lined up. You feel a little awkward but agree anyway. During the week, the job falls through, and although you feel bad about it, you notice that he doesn't make much of an effort to go out and find another.

A week turns into two, and soon you dread coming home after work. You feel like your home is no longer your own. You resent the position you find yourself in, yet feel guilty about being so selfish. After all, the guy has nowhere to go. Then you walk into your house and, once again, find Eddie sitting in your lounger, drinking your beer, and watching your TV . . .

Freeze-frame. I could go on, but you get the picture. What's the surface situation here?

The herd mentality says that poor Eddie has caught a bad break, and since he's your friend, you owe it to him to help him out. You've been lucky, while Eddie has fallen on misfortune. There you sit in a beautiful big home, with a lovely landscaped yard, and he has nothing. Not only is he unemployed, but now his car has broken down, and he doesn't have the money to fix it. He couldn't get a new car because the bank wouldn't approve his credit. As Eddie says, "They only lend money to people that don't need it."

He's having a hard time getting a job because he needs to be paid cash since creditors are hounding him and would garnish his paycheck. His first wife is also harassing him for unpaid alimony and child support.

The truth is, you have a little money saved. You have a car and a house. You have a good job, and you'll get another paycheck this Friday. Eddie hasn't a penny to his name. He *needs* money. You don't. And you probably feel guilty, because you have so much, and Eddie has so little.

This is exactly what moochers like Eddie count on to take advantage of you—using your guilt to manipulate you. But let's look a little deeper.

Five years ago, you and Eddie worked at the same place. He was out the door every day at five sharp. "We're on salary," he had said, "You don't get paid extra to stay late." But you stayed late many times anyway, because you had projects to finish and you wanted a clean desk in the morning. Eddie got a head start on happy hour at the bar.

When there were extra projects to do, you volunteered for them.

Eddie told you that you were stupid for doing so. When time for raises and promotions came, you got them. Eddie quit after a year because the bosses were "cheap, and they play favorites."

Each month, you set aside a little money for savings and your house fund. Eddie couldn't do this because he wasn't "making enough money." His priorities were nightlife at the clubs, cigarettes, getting a flat-screen TV, cable, and the other "necessities" of life.

You went without cable to put the extra $30 a month into your retirement plan. Instead of paying 10 bucks to see a movie when it first came out, you usually paid just three dollars for the video version later. You didn't buy a TiVo because you thought the money was better put in your savings account. You lived on less than what you made and invested the balance in your future.

The herd would tell you that "Poor Eddie can't catch a break." In reality, all the strikes against him are self-created. The situation he is in right now is the result of thousands of little choices he made every day.

He spent eight bucks a day on cigarettes because "The damn tobacco companies got me addicted." He bought a 12-pack of beer twice a week because he "needed to relax." The reason his ex-wife is after him is because he hasn't paid child support payments in two years. The reason the bank won't finance a new car was because he has a legal judgment against him for the student loans he took out and never paid off after he dropped out of college.

He has always spent more than he earned, and now when he is facing a setback, he has no resources to fall back on. So he develops an entitlement mentality. The victimhood role he is playing causes others to feel guilty, and thus they are constantly bailing him out from one scrape after another. He learns how to manipulate his tragedies for maximum effect.

Of course, all the time he is owning this victimhood; he is programming his subconscious mind to attract more drama, more tragedy, and more challenges. He has learned that he can ignore universal laws and live for the moment, because there is always someone to save him from paying the price. So he continues in an endless victim cycle, perpetually getting laid off, left out, and wronged — and forever using others to prevent him from having to take personal responsibility.

So what's the right thing to do? Should you help him? Maybe. But before we address that, let's look at what is going to happen anyway.

Today's social system is ready to catch Eddie in its safety net. The government will feed, clothe, and house Eddie. It will locate job openings for him, set up interviews, and even provide vocational training. It has dozens of social programs for countless contingencies, and it can fund all of them because it forces you to contribute from your paycheck each week. If you refuse, it will put you in prison.

What if, instead of paying your taxes to the government on payday, things went like this: You receive your paycheck and, depending on where you live in the world, you immediately cut a check for 35, 58, maybe even 62 percent of your wages, which would normally represent your income taxes, and you hop into your average sedan and head on over to Eddie's. Eddie is on his porch sipping a can of beer, and he eyes you malevolently as you pull up. Hopping enthusiastically out of your car, you approach him, check in hand.

"Hey, Eddie!" you say. "Just thought I'd drop by with your check seeing as how I was on my way home. There you go, another month of food, clothing, medical and dental care, and entertainment. And because of the raise I received last week, there's a little extra in there for your pension. Well, I can see you're . . . uh . . . busy, so is there anything else I can do for you? No? Well, I'll be off then, I have a ton of paperwork to clear up tonight! Have a wonderful evening, Eddie! Take it easy, and I'll see you next month!"

Would you ever agree to such a thing? In reality, you already have, because that's how the governmental taxation system works. It is currently set up so that the productive people are penalized and the unproductive people are rewarded.

The end result of this dysfunctional system is that it tears down both parties: the people forced to take care of others, and the people receiving the handouts. Of course, the prevalent meme infecting most people is that of chastising the wealthy, believing they create their riches on the backs of the poor. But that's just more bullshit propaganda, designed to make you feel guilty for your success, so that guilt can be used to manipulate you.

Sacrificing yourself and your values for others, whether to gain a sense of moral satisfaction or to escape a sense of guilt, weakens your resolve. Your confidence falters, you may question your own worth, and you end up feeling guilty when you do things to take care of yourself.

I was recently on the phone with a friend of mine who is a general manager at a restaurant. He had just fired a waiter who had worked at the restaurant for nine years. The waiter was supposed to be at work at six on Sunday morning. He called at 5:50 to say he was sick. He was supposed to report Monday morning at seven. He never showed up or even called. He arrived for a staff meeting on Tuesday and was disrespectful and disruptive. It became apparent that he has gone back to using drugs. So my friend fired him, even though he was a long-time friend.

Many people would say this was cold and uncaring. Nothing could be further from the truth. Even though my friend felt sick at having to fire this guy, it is this kind of tough love that has the best chance of getting this individual to turn his life around. Enabling dysfunctional behavior only allows it to continue and become progressively worse.

Take a businessman who keeps a terrible employee because he feels sorry for her. He hasn't the heart to fire her because her life is a wreck. Her mother is an alcoholic, her husband's in jail—whatever the current story is—so he enables her self-destructive behavior and lifestyle by keeping her on. However, keeping this employee—against his better judgment, but for the so-called moral good—means his other employees must pick up the slack. They begin to feel resentful and angry. Performance suffers across the board. Even hardworking, dedicated employees start to give less than their best effort, because they see that they are neither treated with respect nor rewarded in proportion to what they contribute. The customer service declines and sales start going down. Now everyone's job is threatened.

But let's say the businessman had done things differently, selfishly, for the betterment of himself and his company. He calls the errant worker into his office and, after explaining why, he lets her go.

This could be the wake-up call she needs to reevaluate her life and approach. She looks for a job better suited to her skills that she can do well. Or she repeats that same subpar performance, and hopefully gets fired again, so she has another chance to learn the lesson she needs to learn. And just as important, our original boss has a company that isn't in jeopardy and a happy crew to work with.

Equally destructive is the wife who covers for the abuses of her husband, who subjects her with a steady torrent of emotional and physical terror. She spends her whole life walking on eggshells, afraid to call him out. She does him no favors. They both end up living lives of misery.

Imagine though, if she had been strong in her resolve, had confidence in her own values, and had walked away after the first abuse. She would have selfishly saved herself a life of despair rather than live as a sacrificial animal at the hand of a monster.

In a free society, where the needs of the individual come first, people are liberated from guilt and anxiety. Self-sacrifice is more than the root of low self-esteem; it is anti free enterprise and consequently anti humanity. When the living energy of productive citizens is sucked from them by the parasitic herd, what incentive is there to remain productive?

Every man and woman of integrity should earn their own living in the free trade of value for value with others. This means no free rides. No pride can be found in receiving the unearned.

My friend Stuart Goldsmith addressed this topic in a newsletter he sent out a while back. It inspired me to write the following.

Imagine this scenario:

You are with me on a flight to Bali for a Mastermind Retreat when we pass through a severe thunderstorm, and the plane goes down into the sea. Because we got off course and the instruments stopped working, the rescuers have no idea where we are and presume we all perished.

Fortunately, everyone survives. All of us, which includes about 20 other families, get in the life rafts and paddle our way to a deserted island. Being so isolated and completely exposed to the elements, we all quickly go about the construction of shelters and huts from the abundance of bamboo and palm fronds around the island. We search out a freshwater source, which we find located halfway up a mountain, a 30-minute hike from our settlement.

Crab, fish, clams, and mussels live in the surrounding sea, and the island has countless palm and fruit trees, so with a little ingenuity and skill, food abounds. All in all, between hunting and gathering, reinforcing our huts, building fires and cooking food—after looking after the survival needs of our families every day—we all fall exhausted into our makeshift beds at night.

Being a small group, we soon find that by working with others, we can get the work done a bit more efficiently. So we all start making deals. I'll go get the water and firewood for my family and yours today, if you will spend the day fixing up the roof of my hut. And, tomorrow, while I spend the day digging clams and collecting coconuts for our two families, you spend the day getting the firewood and the water.

This improves life, but still most of us spend most of our waking hours on daily survival needs. So, one day, while lying on your back feeling completely exhausted after once again sliding back down the 100-foot incline leading to the water source, you come up with a brilliant idea. What if you rig up a pipe system with bamboo shafts thereby bringing the water to the camp and saving yourself the agony of hauling water?

It's a great idea, just the kind of innovation that can improve life. But how on earth are you going to have the time for such a huge project while you have to worry about the daily grind of feeding and sheltering your family? You decide to work more. While everyone else is resting at night, you labor an extra two hours, building your pipeline. After weeks of strenuous effort, you're finally done.

That evening around the campfire, you call together all the members of the village and make the following proposal:

"Every day you spend your morning trudging up the mountain to bring back water. I have designed and built a pipeline that brings the water directly to the village. I am willing to trade it for fish, coconuts, clothing, and other products of your labor. In a fair exchange of values, we can trade. You win, because you don't have to spend an hour each day

going for water and back. I win, because I don't have to spend so much time fishing, hunting, and farming. All you have to do is walk from your hut to my little water station here and pour yourself some refreshing mountain bubbly!"

In exchange for the use of your pipeline, each family agrees to trade you just 30 minutes of labor (collecting berries, fishing, giving you a massage, etc.), and they get unlimited water, which saves them an hour a day. Yet you receive plenty of everything you need. Everybody wins, because this innovation allowed you to improve the standard of living for the whole village.

Your motivation was selfish, yet you benefited everyone in the community. You were creative and put out the extra effort. It wasn't easy for you to haul bamboo all over the mountain, to fit it and bind it, but you had the idea, and you made the sacrifice to do the work.

Your idea turns out to be so successful, you find yourself with a surplus of many things you receive in trade. So you decide to open up a "7-Eight" store, which is open each evening from seven to eight. You barter the excess goods you have for other things. You continue to trade and collect more things. Pretty soon, you're putting on a new addition to your hut. You add a billiard room and build a deck out back. Next thing you know, you've added a three-bike garage and built a pool in the backyard. You are reaping the reward of your labor and innovation.

Notice that no one was forced into this agreement. If they don't want to trade a half hour of labor with you, they can continue to climb the mountain and fetch their own water each day. Of course no one does, because that would be foolish, costing them extra time and effort.

Inspired by your invention and initiative, your neighbor Fred decides to use the time he's saved by not having to collect water each day to build a boat from a hollowed-out tree. He can now sail out to the deeper water where the big fish swim. He fashions a net by weaving palm fronds and snares many fish at a time, instead of waiting for the few to come in *around the rocks and trying to spear them one at a time. He has so much extra fish to trade he opens Fred's Fish House, with an all-you-can-eat fish fry every Friday night.*

The fish is delicious, and the fish fry turns into "the place to be" every week. It gets so busy that Fred hires the lady from hut six to help him serve everybody. He hires the guy from hut 11 to mix pineapple and mango coolers. Pretty soon he has 10 people from the village working for him. This part-time work earns them some extra coconuts, which they can trade with others to get the goods and services they need.

Meanwhile, Fred's restaurant does so well, he opens a new one at a second location on the other side of the village. As the founder of the island's first successful restaurant chain, he becomes a motivational speaker. His inspirational, you-can-do-this-too "rags to rattan" story inspires millions (okay, dozens) of people all over the world (okay, all over the island).

Fred is so successful now, he can lounge around eating grapes all day. You and Fred design a golf course to occupy your afternoons. He takes up playing conga drums made of coconuts, and you squeeze out some different colored berries and start to paint landscapes. It is the beginning of the arts on your little island.

Possibilities in paradise surround you. Of course, the other families, who have yet to make time-saving innovations of their own, see things a little differently . . .

In fact, they seem to have forgotten that the two of you have saved them hours of time and work with your inventions. They see you lounging in your hammock, while they're out grubbing for berries. They become jealous and resentful, because "it's not fair."

They call a town meeting and decide to elect a government. One of the discontented, Bud, runs on a "populist for the people" platform, and he's elected in a landslide, 98 to 2. Bud immediately introduces a socialist system "for the good of the many." Naturally, he needs to pay himself, as well as hire inspectors for the water pipeline, bureaucrats to license the fishing boat, laborers to sweep the dirt floor at the new city hall, and so on, so they start an income tax system.

Village members start to grumble. This doesn't look so good. They don't like the idea of paying taxes.

Then the new mayor announces that everyone has a right to water and big fish, so he's going to nationalize the pipeline and fishing industry. The government seizes your pipeline; Fred's boat is confiscated as well. Now the villagers are nodding along in agreement. They realize that they no longer have to trade away their labor to you and Fred. The government is going to provide for them. They don't mind paying their taxes, because they realize that this allows them to tax their way into the wallets of the rich people.

This is the beginning of the end . . .

In this scenario, the uninspired islanders would, out of resentment, "seize the means of production" in the name of the public. If you resisted, you would be imprisoned or executed as an "enemy of the state." The herd would be happy, because now they have free access to the water and fishing boat. (Of course, it's not free, but they get more back for their taxes than they pay in, so they couldn't care less.)

But what would happen next?

Kathy, who had an idea how to harness wind and solar power for electricity would figure, "Why bother?" Fernando, who had an idea for a coconut husker, would think the same thing. They would rightly conclude that the extra labor and resources they devote to innovation would never be rewarded, because the government would steal the excess they created and distribute it to the moochers. Progress and innovation would stop.

Cures for diseases would never be found, inventions would never be created, and life would continue to be a primitive struggle for survival. In fact, because there is no reward for free thinking, innovation, or initiative, *eventually the little collective would shrivel up and die or be torn asunder with internal strife.*

Now why am I telling you all this?

It's not to discuss the politics of the situation, as fascinating as that may be. It's to help you realize we are up against a mass of people who want something for nothing—and governments around the world who want to give it to them. Your government wants and needs you to be a worker drone in the collective to support their system in harvesting wealth from the productive people and distributing it to the unproductive—which solidifies their power base. This will be accompanied with all kinds of propaganda about "the greater good" and your "responsibility to take care of those less fortunate than you."

So now you have the herd, organized religion, and the government all telling you to be selfless and take care of others. And if you buy into this crazy shit, you are doomed to a life of lack, misery, and frustration; of unrealized dreams, and settling for mediocrity.

Adopting self-sacrifice as a virtue enables others to take complete advantage of you and, practiced long enough, selfless behavior ultimately destroys you. You have no purpose in life, other than placating others and seeking their approval—which you can only earn by giving up your own happiness. This is sick, twisted, and dysfunctional, but it is what a lot of forces will be trying to program you to do.

I know. I tried to please others for 30 years. But that kind of mindset broke down when my restaurant was seized by the tax authorities and auctioned off at the courthouse. You see, until then, I kept trying to hold it together. I wanted my employees to like me. But they didn't trust me, because I was the rich guy they worked for. Of course, I was anything but rich at that time, but from their perspective I seemed quite wealthy.

They wanted me to give them more raises and benefits. I kept explaining that I was losing money. They responded by saying I could afford to, because I was rich. Besides, they "needed" to earn more money.

Meanwhile, the coalition of local, state, and federal governments kept insisting I needed to pay more in taxes. But if I paid what the government asked for, I couldn't pay more money to my employees. So I dug into the tax money to meet my payroll. And you know where that landed me.

But an interesting thing happened. Once I had lost the restaurant and was broke, my former employees—the ones who had never liked or trusted me because I was supposedly so rich—suddenly liked and trusted me now. I had become one of the group, because I had joined their fraternity of victims.

This was a very important lesson for me. I had given everything I had left to my employees, and I had provided nothing for myself. I had incurred enough debt to keep me in the hole for 10 years. I had done everything I could to take care of the so-called greater good. But when that bled me dry, the greater good was nowhere around to bail me out. All the employees I'd sacrificed everything for had moved on to the next meal ticket.

So I learned the hard way that you must take care of your own needs first. And as I learned more about prosperity and success, I discovered that not only must you be concerned with self-interest, but you must be grounded with a purpose that is congruent for you.

It all begins with your fundamental, core values, the things that are the most important to you, as this drives the actions you take every day. And these spring forth from your central purpose in life—which immediately tells you why the herd goes through their entire lives dumb, sick, and broke.

Now I don't say that to be mean or arrogant, but simply to acknowledge reality. Most people struggle through life simply reacting to events around them, oblivious to the fact that they help create those events. Like a ship tossed at sea, they see themselves buffeted by external circumstances, a tiny object subject to the wrath of the universe, powerless to control the forces around them.

Most people are nowhere near ideal health. In fact, you could conservatively estimate that 90 percent of them suffer from obesity, low energy, disease, or a combination of these.

Most people are nowhere near wealthy. That may sound crass, in light of how much prosperity there appears to be in developed countries like the United States, Europe, Asia, and many other places. And there is no doubt that a great deal of progress has been made. Most people considered poor in these areas not only have the basics—food, shelter, and clothing—but also indoor plumbing, electricity, telephone service, heating, air conditioning, and, of course, TV.

But, while they are wildly rich by the standards of the Third World, the truth is that many of these people are just one hospital bill or a two-week layoff away from bankruptcy. Personal debt has never been higher, while personal savings have never been lower. These people give the appearance of being prosperous, but the reality is that they are broke.

Which brings us to door number three: dumb. Just the fact that most people live their lives sick and broke lets us know they're not rocket scientists.

Now, in the interest of full disclosure, I'm not really as insensitive as I probably appear to be. I'm not happy that those people live that way. And while I agree many were born as victims of circumstances, I don't believe they have to stay that way.

I myself was born dumb, sick, and broke and lived a long time in that reality. But I ultimately prevailed in rising above it, and I believe anyone can do the same. And that is why I write this now and do the work that I do. I want people to seize the prosperity that is their birthright.

I call people dumb in this book a lot, but really that's just a marketing strategy. It gives the media something controversial to flog, and ultimately that gets this message out to millions of people who need it.

Most people are not dumb. They are simply ignorant of what is available for them, just as I was all of those years. I want you and them to taste the life of health, abundance, and intellectual stimulation. To look forward to each and every day with eager anticipation, passion, and joy.

To do that, however, may take having a dramatic shift in your mind-set, beliefs, and opinion of life. It may mean developing a life purpose for the first time, or replacing the one you have right now. And that may mean you have to dramatically alter the view you have of yourself and your role in the world. If you're like most sick, broke, and ignorant people, you define yourself by your roles (husband, engineer, symphony board member, etc.), and you view your purpose through the eyes of servicing others, contributing to the greater good, or looking after the people around you.

And that is insane!

If you define yourself by your roles (Ray's wife, Becky's husband, director of human resources, etc.), then you have no personal identity—which means you have low self-esteem and a low opinion of yourself.

And if you see your main purpose in life as serving others, you're probably personally responsible for the founding of at least three chapters of Co-Dependents Anonymous. Let me go on the record and say, if your main purpose in life is to serve others, then you have an extremely low opinion of yourself, don't believe you are worthy, and will experience a tremendous amount of lack and limitation in your life. And if you tell me that your only purpose here on earth is to "serve God," I think you ought to be in a straightjacket.

Perhaps you think I'm just a materialistic heathen and might reply to what I say here with a statement like, "Really, I don't need all those outside things to be happy. I don't care about money and material things. A car just gets you from point A to point B. I am happy to live in a hut in the rainforest and teach the native people about Christianity. If I get enough grubs to eat, and have a thatched roof over my head, I am satisfied. I am serving others, which is the noble thing. I am doing God's work, and I will be rewarded in the afterlife."

If you feel that way after everything you've read so far, stop reading now. You're so far gone, there is nothing I can do for you. Sell all of your possessions immediately and commit to life as an ascetic.

Frankly, I think you're nuts, but I respect your right to be so.

I would define *insanity* as unsoundness of mind that renders a person unfit to look after his or her own needs for emotional well-being and survival.

People who spend their existence worrying solely about the needs of others and not themselves are not noble, benevolent, and spiritual. They are just crazy. And because they don't look after their own needs first, they really can't help others in a healthy way. They can console them, participate in their drama, or enable their codependence, but they can't offer them real, meaningful help.

Or to repeat an oft-quoted line from a character from Ayn Rand's *The Fountainhead*, "To say 'I love you,' one must first know how to say the word 'I.' "

You know that to love anyone else, you must first love yourself. But are you really aware of what that means on a practical application level? Rand taught that you must live your life by three fundamental values:

1. Purpose
2. Reason
3. Self-esteem

Now let's tie these together with our discussion on selfishness, meeting your own needs first, and creating a life of happiness.

I believe your highest moral purpose must be your own happiness. This is the only healthy, sane way to live, and the only way that ensures the survival of the species and the well-being of the most people. In fact, it is the only honorable way to conduct any relationship!

You must not sacrifice yourself to others, because that is depravity. It is depravity because it fosters a certain state of moral corruption and degradation. It is sick, a sure symptom of mental illness. Do you really get that?

And likewise for the opposite situation: You shouldn't ask others to sacrifice for you, for that is no less sick and depraved. Corrupting the morals of others is no less evil than corrupting your own.

It doesn't serve anyone to degrade yourself or to degrade others. And that is exactly what sacrificing yourself for others is: self-degradation. In the book *Atlas Shrugged*, one of Ayn Rand's main characters is asked, "What is the most depraved kind of human being?" His answer would likely surprise most people, since he doesn't suggest a murderer, or rapist, or other sex offender. His answer is "The man without a purpose."

Later, Rand was interviewed in a watershed article in *Playboy* magazine. When asked why she suggested this as opposed to the other possibilities, she replied, "Because that aspect of their character lies at the root of and causes all the evils which you mentioned in your question. Sadism, dictatorship, or any form of evil is the consequence of a man's evasion of reality. A consequence of his failure to think. The man without a purpose is a man who drifts at the mercy of random feelings or unidentified urges and is capable of any evil, because he is totally out of control of his own life. In order to have control of your life, you have to have a purpose—a productive purpose."*

When you have your own happiness as your highest moral purpose, you have a productive—and moral—reason to exist. And here's the important thing: If *everyone* did this, the world would be a much better place! Instead of dysfunction, depravity, and codependence, we would have healthy, functional, value-for-value relationships. No one would be asked to sacrifice themselves for anyone else. That is the way healthy relationships are created and cultivated.

The next important fundamental value is running your life by reason. Which means that you analyze things within the criteria of whether it serves your highest moral purpose, which is the perpetuation of your happiness.

The question people ask me the most is, "How do I know whether a belief I have is lack-oriented?" This is actually quite easy. The question to ask is simply: "Does this belief serve me?"

---

*From www.ellensplace.net/ar_pboy.html.

The Merits of Selfishness

And the way to discern that is with your rational mind. Emotions are good. They are a vital part of living a full and rich life. But the truly sane and emotionally balanced person will know—or will make it a point to discover—what is causing those emotions. There does not have to be a clash between your emotions and reason.

Yes, you should allow yourself to experience emotions. But don't make life-altering decisions based solely on their influence. Feel your emotions, then learn what causes them. Then use your rational mind to decide what is in your highest good.

That means you extend the situation to its logical conclusion and see if the logic holds up—meaning, check and make sure pursuing a particular course of action to its completion will make you happy. If not, it is counterproductive to your existence. This, of course, leads us to the third fundamental value: self-esteem.

Sane people accept themselves and are comfortable in their own skin. And they are also comfortable with being selfish and ensuring their own needs are met. They understand that if they sacrifice themselves for others, they will diminish and degrade themselves, and ultimately be of use to no one.

Now this leads us to the next question that arises for many. Namely, what about love and relationships?

Love is an expression of your self-esteem, and an expression of your deepest values. You fall in love with someone who shares these values. And if you truly do love someone, it means they bring happiness to your life. Or in other words, *you love them for purely selfish and personal reasons!* If you weren't in love for this reason, it wouldn't make sense. If you were in love for a selfless reason, it would mean that you would get no joy or personal pleasure, that you were in the relationship simply out of self-sacrificial pity for that person. That is not love. It is dysfunctional craziness.

That doesn't mean there aren't millions of people who would accept that kind of sick, superficial love. There are. But those are the people who want to remain dumb, sick, and broke. They merely want to suck the joy, life, and energy from your body. Then, when you are as lifeless as they are, they will be content to know that you share an equal misery.

In a healthy relationship, you choose the person you love, and you fall in love with them because they bring happiness to your life. This is the highest compliment and honor you can ever pay another human being—that you love them for the selfish reason of the happiness and joy they bring you.

Now, all this is not to be confused with hedonism. The philosophy of hedonism teaches that only what is pleasant or has pleasant consequences is intrinsically good. The psychology of hedonism holds that all behavior is motivated by the desire for pleasure and the avoidance of pain. This would seem to suggest that pleasure is a standard for morality, which is most certainly not the case.

That would mean that whatever values you had would be moral. It wouldn't matter if you chose them consciously or unconsciously, with reason or by emotion. You would be basing your morality on whims, urges, or whatever desires possessed you at the moment. This is definitely *amoral*.

Good must be defined by a rational standard of value. Pleasure is not a first cause, but rather a consequence—the consequence of actions you take because you have made a rational value judgment.

Let's continue with this logical exploration of this philosophy to live life by. At this stage many people will ask about serving others and giving to charity. They wonder if I mean that they shouldn't help others or support charities. This is most definitely not what I'm saying. However, there is a belief (often fostered by governments and organized religion) that you have a moral obligation to help those less fortunate than you. Nothing could be further from the truth. This is another belief that keeps people dumb, sick, and broke.

If you live your life by the principles we are discussing, you very well may help others and contribute to charity. Personally, the number one deduction on my tax return for the last 10 years or so has been charity. I anticipate it will remain so for the rest of my life. And I have often helped others with support, even though no one else knows of it, and I don't get a tax credit. But here are the three criteria I use:

1. The person or organization is worthy of the support.
2. I can afford to do it.
3. It brings me happiness to do it.

That alone is what determines on whom and where I spend my charity dollars. It certainly has nothing to do with who is the "neediest" or what causes are politically correct.

I support a great number of causes—the opera, the symphony, my church, wildlife funds, disease prevention and cures, homeless shelters, runaway shelters, and various scholarships. I have bought computers for aspiring entrepreneurs, performance clothing for upcoming singers, and martial arts training for foster kids. I have funded academic scholarships, sponsored more amateur sports teams than I can count, and bought holiday presents for hundreds of kids who wouldn't have gotten any.

But I did this for *purely selfish reasons*! For the happiness it brought me.

And that is where this all leads to. You know exactly what brings value to you and furthers your purpose, which is a life of happiness. It means accepting that you are supposed to be happy and working toward that end, without guilt. Rejecting the herd mentality surrounding you and refusing to give in to schemes and scams that prey on your guilt.

Author and deep thinker Ian Percy raises an interesting point about why so many people don't have a purpose in life. He believes they shy away from getting one because they think it is selfish and all about them. Of course, that's the only thing your purpose can be about!

Ian says, "Knowing your own purpose is the greatest thing you can do for yourself—*simultaneously* and *synergistically* there is no greater way to serve others. The problem is people think they should be subservient to others *without* knowing their own purpose—and that's what drains their soul and ruins their lives. For example, if you help the homeless without that being relevant to your life's purpose, you will feel drained and taken advantage of. Do that same activity because it connects to your life's purpose and it will energize and reward you."

As you look around the world today, it is easy to view man as a helpless, subservient robot. Most people are just worker drones in the collective, living their lives of quiet desperation. We are surrounded by mediocrity, depravity, and fear. But if you look a little deeper, you see something else.

You see the heroism of someone like Bill Cosby, standing up to tell truth. Witness Michael Jordan defy the laws of gravity. Marvel at the triumph of humankind's vision in the Great Pyramids, the Golden Gate Bridge, and skyscrapers to the clouds. You experience one of Puccini's operas, Hemingway's books, or Prince's songs. You stand in awe at the courage of a young athlete paralyzed in an accident, someone battling cancer, or a single mother raising her children alone.

You begin to recognize the enormity of the human spirit, and the greatness we are capable of. You realize that man is not inherently weak and helpless; he just becomes that way when he refuses to use his mind.

And you recognize that you yourself can do great things, and do them for the right reasons. You can be bold, daring, and imaginative, and live a life of health, happiness, and abundance, all while leaving this world a better place because you walked upon it for a while. You can do all this and more when you live your life with purpose.

But there is another element that is vital to purpose: philosophy. Which is what we will explore next.

CHAPTER 10

Philosophy for a Prosperous Life

■ ■ ■

The Power of Congruency

■ ■ ■

One of the most important elements of a prosperous life is living with congruency. This means doing what will take you where you want to be (your highest purpose), operating with integrity (the principles important to you), and standing for something you believe in (values dear to you).

To learn how to do this in life, we're going to have to get philosophical. We need to explore the relationship between philosophy, purpose, principles, and values. These are all familiar words, but let's be sure we know what we're talking about here.

Though they are hard to distinguish, values and principles form the foundation of everything, so let's start there. Your *values* describe how you think the world should work if everything was ideal or perfect. And in fact, even though the world is not perfect, you are *still* going to live your life according to those values.

Principles are the ways in which you are going to apply values in your life. In other words, they are moral or ethical standards by which your actual *behavior* can be measured. So if gratitude is a value of yours, a principle could be that you faithfully tithe at your church.

In order to be true, both values and principles are pretty well unwavering and set in stone. Major events can change them (ask anyone who's had a near death experience or a baby), but if they change with the winds, on a whim, or for convenience you've got a whole other set of problems.

Your life's *purpose* is how you are going to make the world a better place by helping it function more in keeping with your values and ideals. Your purpose is not a state of being; it's what you are actually going to put forth with your life.

Think of it this way: The world is a huge potluck supper. You *value* wholesome, nourishing vegetables more than anything and wish more people did instead of eating junk food. So your *principle* is that you will only bring something vegetarian to the pot-luck supper. Your *purpose* in doing that is to show people how truly delicious a great vegetable dish can be and maybe get others to cut back on the carbs and sugars that are making them big fat slobs.

If everyone had their own happiness as a foundational value, and acted on principles that enabled them to be truly happy, what a wonderful world it would be!

We're still left with this thing called *philosophy*. I define this as a logical system of thought—critical thinking—about the nature, causes, and principles of something. In this case, we are talking about a philosophy for a successful life.

Put another way, your philosophy is your values, principles, and purpose all bundled together. It's the bow around the present. To achieve your purpose in life, and remain true to it, you must live by a congruent philosophy. Everything must be in alignment. Your philosophy describes your purpose, which is based on your principles, which are founded on your values. All of this makes up who you really are.

Analyze anyone's behavior and you end up with their actual values and principles for life—not what they say their principles are, but what they *really* are. Put another way, you believe only what you practice. Anything else is just talk. If someone who believes X also behaves X, we say they are living a congruent life. That doesn't mean they have a prosperous life, just a congruent one. But that's a good start—now we just have to go for prosperity as well.

Everyone lives by principles, whether you like their principles or not. A principle can be "screw the other guy before he screws you" or it can be the Golden Rule, but they are both principles. The same is true for values. Some guys value a woman who is intelligent, articulate, and loving. Other guys value a chick with blonde hair and big breasts. You may think one of these guys is a disgusting chauvinistic pig, but you can't say they have no values.

The memes you've been programmed with determine the values you hold dear, the principles you believe in, and the behavior you practice. For instance, if you are infected with the meme that rich people lie, cheat, and steal, you will approach a partnership with a wealthy person with the intent to get the best of them, before they get you. You wouldn't value integrity, because you'd see no practical application for it. In fact, you'd probably value the art of subterfuge much more in this scenario.

Now you may think that this seems contradictory, wondering why would someone who thinks rich people lie and cheat and steal want to imitate them. But that goes back to the conflict we discussed in Chapter 1. Having a conscious mind that wants one thing, and a subconscious mind working in complete opposition to it.

So if you want to live a prosperous life, you must examine what you believe—the principles on which you base your actual behavior. If those principles are not useful in taking you to your higher purpose (happiness), then look at what needs to change and how to change it, because you always have the free will to do so. Once you have your life's principles clear, then you live your life (make choices) in a way that is congruent and aligned with those principles.

Now if you long for prosperity, you must make choices aligned with principles that are congruent with prosperity—meaning they are based on integrity and value-for-value exchange.

Today we live in a very complex world, and this world challenges our principles like nothing ever before. The Middle East conflict, free trade issues, human rights abuses, stem cell research, and cloning are all examples of the modern-day complexities that can cause us to question our principles. Each year progress and technology create new and intricate political, philosophical, and intellectual dilemmas.

In response to this, politicians, the media, and society in general often talk of compromise. They would have you believe that today's world is now so difficult to deal with that values and principles no longer work. They argue that we must all compromise more, so that everyone can benefit. This is like sticking your feet in the freezer and your head in the oven, to get to the middle ground on warm.

Compromising on principles is a big reason so many people are so messed up. Because only your ability to form principles allows you to deal effectively and positively with the challenges of life today. Your principles are the moral barometer you use to evaluate issues that come before you and decide what your proper behavior should be.

In many cases, when you violate a principle for the sake of compromise, you solve the short-term problem at the expense of creating more complexity, which leads to greater long-term challenges. We can push this even further and say that what this incongruent behavior does is reveal your real values and principles, so in a way there really is no violation at all. Either way you look at it, your *walk* doesn't back up your *talk*. (It exposes the conflict between what you think you want, and what you really want.)

When I opened a direct marketing agency in Central Europe, the first company that approached us about representing them was a tobacco company. Actually, they were the *only* company that approached us. It would have been easy to validate or justify taking this company, especially with no other client in sight. But I didn't consider it for a minute. There is no way on this earth that I am going to create marketing campaigns to promote cigarettes, not even for a multimillion-dollar fee.

If you remember, the way prosperity comes into your life is by filling a vacuum. The vacuum we created by not accepting the tobacco company's business opened up a place for others to come in. But that was irrelevant. If I had to sell cigarettes to make my marketing agency a success, I would rather dig ditches. My philosophy of doing business involves creating value and the highest good for all concerned. I have no problem with tobacco companies selling cigarettes, or with people buying them. I want them to have that free choice. But it wouldn't be congruent with my philosophy for me to be involved with the marketing of tobacco.

When you talk about holding to a principle, most of the herd will start labeling you with words like *stubborn, unreasonable, narrow-minded, unrealistic,* and *rigid*. Then they trot out the argument about the complexities of today's world requiring you to compromise more, be more flexible, and relax your standards.

I'll take my cue from Thoreau and settle for a majority of one. Try this premise on for size:

- To be happy, you must have a purpose.
- To have a purpose requires having personal values.
- Your values create a congruent philosophy to live by.
- Your philosophy is congruent only if you live by the principles that support that philosophy.

It is your rational mind's ability to form principles that gives you the means to deal with complex issues. Your need to act on rational principles is inescapable if you want to live a life of happiness, meaning, and significance. And this is going to require that you use your reason and intellect—not emotion—as you determine the principles by which you live.

Take politics, for example. If you live in the States and consider yourself a Democrat or a Republican, you don't live by prosperity principles. Likewise if you live in Australia or the United Kingdom and vote for the Labour Party or the Conservative Party. And it goes without saying (but won't) that if you believe in socialism or communism, you are anti prosperity as well.

"Now wait a minute," you say. "What's my political affiliation got to do with it? Why are you dragging politics into this, anyway?"

Because your political beliefs will reveal what principles you live by. If you really believe in true prosperity you also understand that it is founded on a couple of unbreakable principles—the most important being private property rights and the right to keep the fruits of your own labor.

And *all* the major political parties around the world, like the Democrats, Republicans, Conservatives, and Labour, violate this principle. They will seize your house by eminent domain and give it to a private developer who wants to build a casino or shopping center, all in the name of the greater good. They will tell you that you can't smoke marijuana in your own home or you must wear a seat belt when you drive your own car. They will seize a percentage of your earnings to fund their social programs for the herd.

Of course, these government officials will claim that they are acting in the interest of society to provide prosperity for all. But these actions violate the principles of private property and your right to keep what you earn—so they are actually anti humanity, and thus anti prosperity.

Now, you have the right to be a Republican or Democrat. But you can't say you have a congruent philosophy for prosperity, because the principles (as reflected in behavior) of those parties are anti prosperity. (This creates the mental conflict discussed in Chapter 1.)

Republicans claim to be the party of small government. But their principles (behavior) of trying to legislate what a woman can do with her body or what consenting adults can do in their own bedroom show that what they really want is to micromanage your life so you meet *their* moral standards.

Democrats claim that they are the party for the little guy, standing up against the wealthy and powerful interests. But the things they champion, like minimum wage laws, workers' comp, antitrust laws, welfare, and a myriad of other regulations, actually work to strangle business growth and jobs, keeping poor people poor.

In fact, the only current political party with a credo consistent with the principles of prosperity is the Libertarian Party. You see, the Libertarian philosophy is simple, yet profound. They maintain you have the right to do anything you want, *provided you do not infringe on the rights of others.*

Want to ride a motorcycle without a helmet or drive your car without your seat belt? No problem. Want to smoke dope or mainline heroin? Not an issue. However, if you rob my house to get the money for your heroin, that is an issue, because now you are trampling on *my* private property rights to exercise your rights. Likewise it's an issue if you try to drive under the influence of heroin, because you might crash into my car or run me over.

My friend Bob Burg makes another interesting point on this: The only reason a heroin addict would need to rob my home to get enough money to pay for his habit is because of the insane war on drugs, which has driven up the price of illegal drugs and provided an incentive for black market sales and corruption—just as Prohibition did for alcohol in the 1920s. Most people think that robbery, violence, and pushers hooking kids on drugs are a natural result of drug use. They are actually the natural result of drug *prohibition*.

Take it another level. Libertarians maintain that the government be charged with only three areas of responsibility:

1. Maintain an army to defend the nation against attack.
2. Manage a police force to protect our rights.
3. Operate a court system to adjudicate disputes.

That's it. That means the government would not run the schools, hospitals, trains, highway system, nor provide a multitude of other services we have come to expect. All those things would be left to the free enterprise system.

This free enterprise model is the only position you can support for government if you live by a congruent philosophy of prosperity for all. Because, as we discussed earlier, most of the benefits government provides—like free prescriptions, public schools, college grants, and so on—are actually done at the expense of the rights of others. At its basic level, this is just a Robin Hood tax on productive people to support the nonproductive ones.

Most people say things like "Education is a basic human right." But that's not true, because the only way you can guarantee everyone an education is to take money at gunpoint (i.e., government taxation under penalty of fines or imprisonment) from others to pay for that education.

Many people will maintain that basic medical care is a human right. But that's not true either, because you're going to either compel the doctors and nurses to work for whatever mandatory salary you set (a violation of their human rights), or you are going to forcibly take money from other people (violating their rights) to pay those doctors and nurses their customary level of compensation.

So what does that mean in a practical application sense? Well, for me, it means that in the next election, I have to vote for the Libertarian candidate, because that political philosophy is congruent with the principles of prosperity and happiness I live by.

"But wait," you say. "Your guy shows only a 1 percent approval rating in the polls. He doesn't have a chance to win."

But that's where the majority of one comes in. If I believe in my principles, I *must* live by them, or I have no moral compass to guide my life, and I will twist in the whipping winds of convenience, peer pressure, and luck.

To be prosperous, you must first be happy. And to be happy, you must first have a purpose, know what it is, and live in a way that is congruent with it—even when doing so is inconvenient, politically incorrect, or unpopular; even when your emotions are pulling you another way.

The first time I conducted my "Sacred Secrets of Prosperity" workshop was in Sydney, Australia. I was delighted to see Peter there, an old friend and a wonderful guy. Peter lives life in a wheelchair. Yet one of the statements I made at that workshop said that if you really believed in the principles of prosperity, then you could never support laws requiring wheelchair access for private businesses, such as hotels, stores, and restaurants. Because requiring a restaurant to do this interferes with the proprietor's private property rights. It forces him to spend additional money to build a ramp, larger bathrooms, and other facilities that perhaps he can't afford.

"But, come on, Randy," you say. "What kind of a mean son-of-a-bitch are you that you would deny Peter the right to eat at the restaurant of his choosing? I mean, it's just a ramp and some safety bars. What's the big deal? People in wheelchairs have the right to eat out just like anyone else."

Actually, that last statement is false. You can't be congruent with prosperity principles if you insist that people in wheelchairs have a right to eat at any restaurant they want, because to do so would run roughshod over the rights of all of those private property restaurant owners.

And remember, if you want to live a life of happiness, then your philosophy must be congruent and be able to be extended to its logical conclusion.

When I raised the issue of forcing restaurants to provide wheelchair access in Sydney, virtually the entire room felt that this was a good law and a correct use of government power. Then I asked if anyone in the audience operated a home-based business. About 45 percent of the hands went up. I asked how many had wheelchair ramps for their customers who might drop by to pick up a product from them. No one did.

Next I asked how many people had web sites to promote their

business. Again almost every hand in the room went up. Then I asked how many of them had audio translations of all the writing on their site, so blind people wouldn't be discriminated against if they surfed onto it. Every hand went down.

"That's going too far," you say. "You're exaggerating to cloud the issue." No, actually, that very antidiscrimination lawsuit is working its way through the U.S. court system right now.

So how congruent is your philosophy? How can you deny the right of a blind person to access all the material on your web site if you believe the wheelchair-bound have the right to visit every other business? Where does your philosophy go if you take it to its logical next level?

When you look at the McDonald's drive-through menu, it states that picture menus are available on request. But did anyone stop to think that illiterate people wouldn't be able to read that helpful message? What about the instructions in braille on the ATM drive-through? They're on there. But did you ever stop to think how a blind person would drive there?

These examples are asinine, but true. They are what happens when you have the government telling people what to do with their private property.

Let's get back to the congruence within your philosophy: If you believe that the government should ensure that no private businesses discriminate against anyone, what is the logical extension of that? The next level means that instead of being able to start up a business selling Avon or Mary Kay for a few hundred dollars, now a person needs wheelchair ramps, an extra bathroom, audio content on their web site, picture menus for the illiterate, sign translators for the deaf, and who knows what else.

Suddenly it takes $50,000 to start a simple home-based business, a hot dog cart, or a lemonade stand. The cost of entry is so high it sails out of the reach of the majority of people. The result is that innovation slows down, many jobs are never created, and everyone suffers. And it actually hurts the poor people and the people with physical challenges the most!

The cost of the entrance level fee for going into any business becomes so high that the only people who can afford to do it are those who are already wealthy. Poor people would be stuck with one option—that of always working for richer people. And people with any kind of physical challenge would actually have far fewer choices, because competition would be reduced so greatly.

Now the emotion in me wants Peter (or my friend W. Mitchell) to be able to go to lunch with me at whatever restaurant they want to eat at and not have to worry whether their wheelchair will fit. But I have to rise above that emotion and look at the principle involved. And it's just not right that the government tells private restaurant owners that they have to have handicap access on their property.

If you have a congruent philosophy of happiness and prosperity, you have to defend the private property owner's right not to spend that extra money. It's probably a bad decision for that person, marketing-wise, but you have to defend their right to make bad decisions for their own private property.

This also means that you support their right to put a "No fags," "We don't serve Jews," or "No Asians allowed" sign in their window as well. Because if they spend $100,000 building a restaurant on their own private property, they have the right to serve whom they want—and only whom they want. You do not have the right to eat there just because you want to, if your right can only be accommodated by infringing on their right.

Don't get me wrong. I think it would be absolutely abhorrent for someone to do this, and such actions would certainly reflect lack thinking on their part. But the philosophy I live by requires me to support their right to choose the customers they want to serve.

"But wait," you say. "How will people in wheelchairs (or gays, Asians, etc.) eat?" The answer is simple: Get the government out of the equation, and the free market will take care of itself.

Smart restaurants and hotels would figure out that it is good business to have handicapped access so they can serve a larger clientele and thus increase profits. Internet sites and associations would develop to let people in specific communities know where they could find restaurants and hotels that cater to their needs. This is already happening for people who have pets. Before taking a trip, they go online and discover all the properties along the way where both they and their pets are welcome.

I think you will see the same kind of thing happening next for people who smoke. There are so many smoke-free places now, that a strong niche market will develop for places that cater to smokers—except for one problem: The government keeps legislating what people can do with their private property, and soon no hotels will be allowed to let people smoke on the premises if the current trend continues.

Now again, rise above the emotion and look at the principle involved. I don't smoke, and I don't want to eat next to someone smoking, and I don't want a hotel room that smells like an ashtray. But I would absolutely defend a private hotel owner's right to offer smoking facilities if they desired, because if you let the government curb their rights, yours will be next.

Antidiscrimination laws for private business and private property are actually anti humanity, and thus anti prosperity.

Public property is a different story. When the government builds a post office, hospital, or highway, these must be accessible to everyone, because everyone helped pay for them. (But, of course I believe the government shouldn't be building a post office, hospital, or highway.)

Now let's take your philosophy even further to test whether it still remains congruent. I'll ask you the same questions I posed to my prosperity students in Sydney:

I asked how many people thought prostitution should be legalized. Maybe three-quarters of the room agreed. (And it is legal in Australia, by the way,) Then I asked how many people thought that all drugs should be legalized. Very few hands went up.

I told that crowd and I will tell you: If you have a congruent philosophy toward prosperity, you absolutely have to support the right of someone to offer sex for money or to be able to pay for sex, and to support the right of someone to sell crack, crystal meth, or marijuana and use those drugs themselves.

The fact that you think drugs are bad is irrelevant. The fact that your religion believes sex shouldn't take place outside of marriage doesn't matter. What matters are the principles your philosophy is grounded on. And happiness and prosperity must be grounded on people's freedom to choose, and their right to do things that please themselves, *as long as this doesn't infringe on the rights of others.*

If you give the government the power to tell you that you can't smoke dope in your house or hire a sex worker, it is only a short step to their banning books, censoring the press, and creating a police state.

If you think the government should provide all children with an education or all seniors with free prescription drugs, or you believe everyone has a right to a good job, you must realize that those "rights" all come at a price. If you think it is your government's job to pass laws to protect you from buying a supplement with ephedrine in it, to prevent you from bungee jumping, or to give you a paycheck when you lose your job—you must realize there is a far more serious price to pay.

The government cannot be responsible for your prosperity, any more than your doctor can be responsible for your health, or your church/temple/synagogue can be responsible for your spirituality. If you want to be prosperous, you have to take responsibility for that yourself.

I strongly suggest you spend some time really thinking about these issues, because they will reveal whether you live your life by a congruent philosophy, or drift about aimlessly, dropping principles whenever they become inconvenient.

Now I'm quite sure someone will accuse me of saying the only way you achieve prosperity is if you vote Libertarian, smoke crack, and hire hookers. And while that may be one interesting way, that's not what I am advocating. What I am trying to do is to shake you out of your comfort zone and get you to think again.

I think Ayn Rand was brilliant—at least 75 years ahead of her time. *Atlas Shrugged, The Fountainhead, Philosophy: Who Needs It,* and *The Virtue of Selfishness* are required reading for anyone who is serious about success and happiness. Yet I don't agree with everything she espoused, and you don't have to either. And frankly, some of the people I see running for office on the Libertarian ticket strike me as kooks. It appears to me that they have lost touch with the founding principles of the party.

And if you just accept everything I say without questioning it, you're just moving from one imprisoning mind-set to another. If you study what I suggest, do some critical thinking, and then develop a belief, you will be on your way to prosperity.

If your beliefs truly serve you, they will survive a healthy, critical questioning. Take some time and explore some of the resources, people, and ideas I have suggested here and decide for yourself. I have created a page offering more information and resources on these topics. You'll find details at the end of the book. Visit the sources there and learn more about what I feel are issues essential to your personal prosperity.

Once you understand the critical importance of values and principles and then develop a congruent philosophy based upon them, you can build a life of purpose, meaning, and happiness. And that's a pretty cool place to be. Now let's talk about how you tie all this together . . .

CHAPTER 11

Putting It All Together for Health, Happiness, and Prosperity

■ ■ ■

Getting Smart, Healthy, and Rich!

■ ■ ■

As I work with people to help them develop their success, wealth, and happiness, I've noticed a common thread running through what they tell me. They come into the work thinking fear of failure is holding them back. Most of the time, we discover it is actually fear of success that is really stopping them.

They are scared that if they become successful, their friends and family won't relate to them any more. They're afraid that if they become rich, they won't get into heaven. They think that obtaining great wealth will bring even greater challenges. They suffer from self-doubt, wondering if becoming successful means they will turn into an uncaring spouse or a bad parent.

They aren't really afraid of failure. They are petrified of succeeding. So subconsciously they do things to sabotage their success.

Fear of success is the by-product of low self-esteem and is a direct result of the programming discussed all throughout this book—the fear you get when you're infected with the core beliefs of the herd. The members of the herd have been told *what* to think for so long, they no longer know *how* to think for themselves.

To break free from herd-think, you must become a critical thinker and a contrarian. You have to question everything. Accept nothing as fact that doesn't lead you toward prosperity, because anything that doesn't lead you there isn't real. It is erroneous information spread by memes. You have to be able to discern the difference.

The reason most people are living lives of quiet desperation is that they are incapable of discernment. The reason Bill Gates is a billionaire is that he can discern things that others can't. He questions things. He wonders, "What if?" "Why?" "Why not?" He is able to discern the difference between doing something because it makes sense and doing it because "everybody does it that way."

Bill Gates is a contrarian. So were Henry Ford, J. Paul Getty, Andrew Carnegie, Leonardo da Vinci, Guglielmo Marconi, Thomas Edison, Albert Einstein, Ayn Rand, and countless other brilliant thinkers throughout history whose names we'll never know. Successful people don't think like the pack. They question everything.

Since we're talking about Bill Gates, let's compare the way he thinks with the way most people do.

Waiting in an airport lounge, I picked up a copy of *Fortune* magazine. It featured a column by Stuart Alsop criticizing Microsoft and Gates. Headlined "The Right Thing to Regulate," this article perpetuated the assertion that Microsoft is a monopoly and spoke in favor of the U.S. government's antitrust action against the company and Gates, its chairman.

This is typical herd thinking. Microsoft and Bill Gates—what an easy target, one that is sure to be popular with the rest of the herd. Most love to accept the opinion that Microsoft is the "death star" of monopolies, destroying everything in its path until it controls the world. And Gates is one of the wealthiest men in the world, so he is the perfect target for the mentality of envy and jealousy.

When Alsop writes a column like this, he shows his lack of understanding of how capitalism and free enterprise actually work, demonstrating how infected with lack memes he really is. And the fact that a magazine like *Fortune*—which is supposed to be an icon of free enterprise—prints such silly socialist nonsense shows you how pervasive lack memes have become.

When someone asked Ayn Rand why Americans are so anti-intellectual, she replied that it was because America's intellectuals were so anti-American. This article is a perfect demonstration of that. A magazine started by one of free enterprises greatest achievers, dedicated to being a forum for thought and ideas to promote the development of the free enterprise system, instead is championing a course of action that would be better suited for a communistic regime.

What exactly is Microsoft's crime? Bill Gates and company have created software millions of people want to use. They have made it possible for people all around the world—people like me who are not especially computer savvy—to use computers to improve our lives in so many ways. But the real "crime," according to the U.S. government, was that Microsoft was bundling its Internet browser with the operating system, therefore strangling trade and creating a monopoly.

Let's take this convoluted logic and apply it in another scenario. Suppose both Anthony Robbins and I are giving seminars on the same weekend in Chicago. I offer a free CD set with each seminar registration. Should Anthony sue me? Petition the government? He could claim unfair trade, restraint of trade, and that I hold a monopoly on my products. Or he could just offer a free CD album with his own seminar. Better yet, he could offer two!

The government does not need to legislate what companies can offer, control their prices, nor determine the value of their products. If you let free enterprise work, it will take care of the consumer all by itself. Competition is what keeps prices low and values high.

If you are serious about success, Bill Gates should be one of the heroes at the top of your list. And Microsoft should be treated by the U.S. government as what it really is—a true American success story.

It's easy to depict Microsoft as the billion-dollar monster, devouring everything in its path. That's what Alsop and the majority of the media would have you think. It's easy pickings, pandering to Joe Lunchbucket. But these attacks ignore one very simple fact.

Microsoft is a company formed by a couple of kids who dropped out of college because they had an idea and a dream. Bill Gates and Paul Allen created a company based on fulfilling a need through innovation, and they attracted people like Richard Brodie and legions of other bright people.

The thing that will ultimately control Microsoft is not government regulation. It is the fact that right now, all over the world, there are other bright kids sitting in a college dorm room somewhere with nothing but empty pizza boxes who will come up with the next development in software, one that could make Word, Excel, Explorer, or even Windows obsolete. And they will do this because they are driven by the desire to live the American dream, as personified by Gates, Allen, and the thousands of millionaires created by Microsoft.

Yet if you read the business and computer trade magazines, you'll slowly become programmed that Microsoft is bad and Gates is the enemy. That's why you have to be discerning. Question what you read and hear. Analyze why the herd thinks the way it does. And think for yourself.

Some years ago, I lived with a woman named Aura Alicia. One day we were sitting on the couch together, and she asked me to hand her purse to her, which was sitting on a chair next to me. She took out what she wanted and handed back the purse, which I set on the floor next to me.

"No, no, no!" she exclaimed.

"What, what, what?" I asked, as I jerked the purse back into my hands.

"The floor is no place for a purse," she replied firmly.

"Oh, I'm sorry," I responded, and I put the purse back on the chair.

A few seconds later, I started laughing. Aura wanted to know what was so funny.

"'The floor is no place for a purse'?" I asked "That sounds like something your grandmother would say. And, besides, please tell me exactly *why* the floor is no place for a purse."

She thought about that for a few seconds and began to laugh herself. She had no idea why the floor was no place for a purse. She just remembered once as a little girl, she put her mother's purse on the floor and received that same admonishment. She never realized that programming was lodged in her subconscious mind until more than 20 years later, when the situation presented itself for her to parrot what she had been told.

We start to learn things before we can even walk, and pretty much have our worldview established by the time we are 10. Most people never realize their view is set and certainly never question it. Successful, happy people *do*.

Not that long ago, cell phones were impossible. When Marconi suggested the radio, people knew he was insane. And Edison? Everyone knew what a crazy idea the light bulb was. Yet "everyone" is often wrong.

I'm convinced that the highest levels of success in sports, in business, and in life come not so much from skill, training, and ability as they do from the mind-set of the person who reaches these levels. Such success often requires thinking contrary to what the herd is thinking, and *always* requires you to question the beliefs you hold—on everything.

When you question your beliefs, you question your limitations. If your beliefs serve you, they can withstand the scrutiny. If they don't survive the questioning, you can drop them and replace them with beliefs that *do* serve you.

Here are some examples: You may have a belief that it's hard to succeed without a college education, that you need money to make money, that doing business in your big city/small town is difficult, and/or that people of your race have a harder time making it.

You may discover that these beliefs do not serve you and decide to replace them with beliefs that do. Some examples of replacement beliefs are:

- Bill Gates and Paul Allen made it without a college education. I can too.
- You need only a great idea to make money.
- People in my city/town have already been successful. That means I can be successful too.
- Many people of my race are successful; no one can keep me down but myself.

By questioning the status quo, you prevent yourself from falling into victim mentality and developing fear, self-doubt, and lack. You recognize selfishness as a virtue and not an evil as the masses believe it to be. You realize that the government playing Robin Hood actually hurts everyone.

These are some pretty big topics we've looked at, and we've really only brushed the surface. Your job is to dig deeper, to study more, to confront your beliefs and question them, because that is where the breakthroughs are. Becoming a critical thinker and developing discernment can take you out of the daily survival grind of the herd and lead you to the intoxicating realm of self-actualization.

I wrote this book to challenge your beliefs, threaten you, and, most importantly, *get you to think!* I don't expect you to accept everything I say as right. If you do, I haven't done my job. But if you think about these issues—engage in real, critical thinking to determine what is right for you—then I have done my assignment.

To create a life of meaning, fulfillment, and prosperity, you have to be open to questioning everything—especially deep-seated beliefs that you feel strongly about. Pay particular attention to things that arouse your emotions. If you get really mad about something you read here—then that is an issue that needs serious reflection on your part. Any mental health professional will tell you that when you react emotionally to an issue, something there threatens you and causes insecurity. We mirror things, and usually something that angers us most about another person is an issue we fear in ourselves.

When you do your self-examination and critical thinking, ask yourself this question:

Am I holding on to certain beliefs because they allow me to validate behavior that is keeping me from my greatness?

That may be the most important question you ask yourself all year, so treat it with the reverence it deserves. I want you to tap into all the greatness you have. And that's why I wrote the book I did. You've honored me by reading it and accepting me as your success coach. That's a responsibility and a covenant that I take very seriously.

A casual friend may tell you want you want to hear, but a true friend or mentor will tell you what you *need* to hear. I could have written one of those feel-good, New Age books filled with warm, loving talk that panders to your existing beliefs. And you would probably have thought it was brilliant. But you would have stayed stuck where you are. This book can help you break through to a lifestyle most people dream about, but never really achieve.

You were born to be healthy, happy, and prosperous. I just wanted to plant that idea with you, because we know that ideas are centers of consciousness. Your health, happiness, relationships, financial situation, and intelligence will all be determined by the thoughts you give precedence to, the ideas you birth in your mind.

Build on your awareness of universal laws and expand your faith in your own innate good as well as the talents you are blessed with. The oppositional stuff will come, and it will come in great abundance. But know that it comes not at your expense, but at your *expanse*. Your faith in right outcomes is the only belief you need.

I believe that faith is a superhuman power we possess—a mind power with the ability to shape substance. The foundation for every work is an idea. Faith makes the idea real to you and your subconscious mind. It even makes it real to others. When others have faith in the thing you are doing, selling, or creating, they see it as worthy of their support. This creates the power of the Mastermind and greatly expands your prosperity power.

God/Universe/Power does not grant your requests. Your prosperity and abundance have been provided for already. You just need to claim what is yours.

There are no miracles, as most people perceive them. Hoping for miracles means believing that you may or may not benefit from some whimsical, capricious act by God/Universe/Power. Instead, expect to receive all you need in its own due and natural course, as you call upon that force.

Your prosperity is not tied to the economy, your job, your education, your boss, or your past. It is here, now, for you to manifest as you choose to. Every person on this planet—you included—deserves to experience abundance. You were born to be rich, healthy, and happy. Now it is up to you to accept what is yours!

You can fight my premises and deny what I have written. You can find thousands who will support you to do this. From your minister to your newspaper editor, from your elected representatives to your best friend, they are lots of people who will tell you that you are the special victim of circumstances. They will seek to discredit me, and validate the reasons for your lack of success and happiness. They will defend to the death your right to be dumb, sick and broke. And you can feel noble for being so.

Or you can take in what I say. Question it, along with your core, foundational beliefs. You can sort through the issues, uncover the subconscious programming you didn't know was there and replace it with positive programming and empowering beliefs. You can actually develop a purpose in your life, and live by a philosophy which supports it. And choose to be smart healthy and rich.

What's it going to be?

Resources

Please use this book as a starting point, and explore more deeply the subjects raised in it. Discover for yourself the ideas that will help you create success. Here are some additional resources to develop your knowledge in these key areas.

For more information on Ayn Rand and her philosophy, visit the Ayn Rand Institute at www.AynRand.org. Her books *The Fountainhead, Atlas Shrugged, Philosophy: Who Needs It,* and *The Virtue of Selfishness* are all brilliant works and required reading for anyone serious about success. The Institute does great work educating new generations about this important work.

For more information on the Libertarian Party and the principles they espouse, visit their web site at www.lp.org. You may also obtain much valuable information from the Center for Small Government. Find them at www.CenterForSmallGovernment.com.

To learn about Prosperity Manifestation Maps, and other resources to help you develop your prosperity consciousness, visit www.ProsperityUniverse.com. I offer a 31-day study program called *The Midas Mentality* that you may want to consider.

If you would like to know more about Network Marketing and training resources in that area, be sure to read my book, *How to Build a Multi-Level Money Machine* (Wichita, KS: Prime Concepts Group, 1998). You can find it along with many other generic training resources at www.NetworkMarketingTimes.com. Be sure to register for the free training e-zine and browse the many training articles there.

Resources

If you would like to get the subliminal programming CDs I recommend, they are from Steven Halpern and can be found at www.innerpeacemusic.com.

To learn about the information entrepreneur business, check out the Home Study program at www.HowToSellInfo.com.

And finally, if you would like to receive my "Randy's Rants" free e-mail newsletter, sign up at my web site, www.RandyGage.com. You'll get a message from me every other week, straight talk on the subjects of success, marketing, and prosperity.